Masculine Compromise

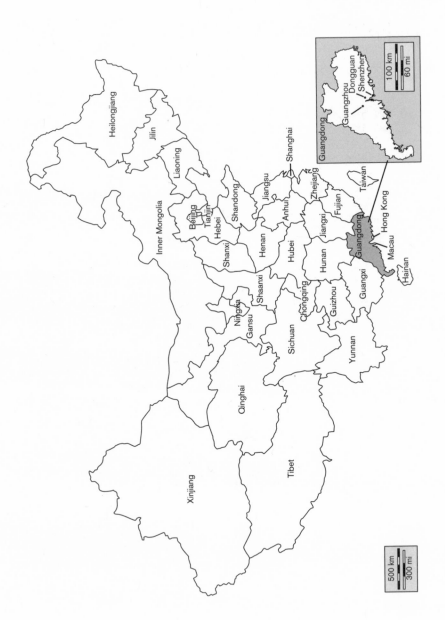

Masculine Compromise

Migration, Family, and Gender in China

Susanne Y. P. Choi and
Yinni Peng

UNIVERSITY OF CALIFORNIA PRESS

University of California Press, one of the most
distinguished university presses in the United States,
enriches lives around the world by advancing scholarship
in the humanities, social sciences, and natural sciences. Its
activities are supported by the UC Press Foundation and
by philanthropic contributions from individuals and
institutions. For more information, visit www.ucpress.edu.

University of California Press
Oakland, California

Library of Congress Cataloging-in-Publication Data

Choi, Susanne Y. P., author.
    Masculine compromise : migration, family, and gender
in China / Susanne Y. P. Choi and Yinni Peng.
        pages   cm
    Includes bibliographical references and index.
    ISBN 978-0-520-28827-0 (cloth : alk. paper)
    ISBN 978-0-520-28828-7 (pbk. : alk. paper)
    ISBN 978-0-520-96325-2 (e-edition)
        1. Rural-urban migration—China, South.
    2. Urban-rural migration—China, South.
    3. Masculinity—Family relationships—China, South.
    4. Gender—China.   5. Migration, Internal—China,
    South.   6. China—Social conditions—1949-   I. Peng,
    Yinni, author.   II. Title.
        HB2114.A3C48   2016
        307.2'40951—dc23   2015028009

Manufactured in the United States of America

24   23   22   21   20   19   18   17   16   15
10   9   8   7   6   5   4   3   2   1

In keeping with a commitment to support
environmentally responsible and sustainable printing
practices, UC Press has printed this book on Natures
Natural, a fiber that contains 30% post-consumer waste
and meets the minimum requirements of ANSI/NISO
Z39.48–1992 (R 1997) (*Permanence of Paper*).

Contents

Acknowledgments

Migration and transnational family have been central parts of Susanne and Yinni's lives. We therefore feel privileged and humbled to have had the opportunity to study these issues in depth. While completing this book we benefited from the generous help, support, and encouragement of a great many people. First and foremost, we are indebted to the migrant workers and families who opened their hearts to us, and shared with us their stories of joy, pain, and hope. We are grateful for their sincerity, straightforwardness, and down-to-earth attitude. Many of those we interviewed wondered why we were interested in their stories. Some suspected that the interviewers were undercover agents sent by the Chinese government, and others asked if we were journalists. Most simply considered their life as a migrant too ordinary to be of any significance to the larger world. This book is a tribute to these "ordinary" migrants—for they did not know that it is their "ordinariness" that has been the foundation of China's spectacular economic growth and rapid development. This book is also a testament to the human cost of that development, the heartache it has meant for China's millions of migrant workers and their families, and the resilience they have demonstrated during their country's grand social transformation.

This book developed out of a larger collaboration with Du Ping. Her insights and ideas were important to the project, and her exceptional interview skills have been invaluable. It would not have been possible to collect the data on which this book is based—interviews with 192 migrant men and 74 migrant women—without the assistance of Li Siran, Luo Ming, Ruby Lai Yuen Shan, Javier Pang Chi Long, Max Li Xiaojun, Katy Chan Pui Man, KC Chao Kin Chong, Jenny Chiu Tuen Yi, Carol Mai Yee Yan, Zhang Kecheng, and Julian Yeung Wing Yan. Their enthusiasm, interview skills, and cheerful personalities were vital to the success of the fieldwork, and they added much energy and laughter to the process. We will always have fond memories of the time we spent in the field—visiting villages in cities, trying out cuisines cooked by migrants from different parts of China, and exploring the streets of Shenzhen, Guangzhou, and Dongguan—as part of our shared sociological journey.

Particular thanks go to Julian for his assistance throughout the data collection process and the writing of the book. We are also grateful for the help our anonymous fieldwork coordinators in China provided. Although we cannot mention them by name, we would like them to know that without their help it would have been much more difficult to gain access to migrant workers, and the logistics of interviewing so many people would have been much more of a challenge. The pictures taken by Tang Chung Wang capture the sentiments, humanity, feelings, and atmosphere of migrant life in a way that is beyond words, and they have added immeasurably to the vividness of the book; we wholeheartedly thank him for his contribution.

In the process of writing this book Susanne was inspired and helped by three great sociologists—Mary Brinton, Pierrette Hondagneu-Sotelo, and Deborah Davis. Mary kindly sponsored Susanne's visit to Harvard University between September and December 2013 as part of her sabbatical. These four precious months allowed Susanne temporarily to leave behind her various academic and family responsibilities in Hong Kong and focus on writing chapters 1, 4, and 5 of the book. Susanne's discussion with Mary encouraged her to think more deeply and boldly about the intersection between migration and gender. Pierrette Hondagneu-Sotelo's work on Latina migrant domestic workers, transnational mothering, gender, and migration have had a great influence on our thinking about migration and gender, so when we met her at a conference in Hong Kong in December 2013, we were thrilled that she very generously offered to read and critique some of the chapters, and recommended the book to the University of California Press. We will be forever indebted to her for this support. Deborah Davis has been one of the kindest yet most meticulous critics of China studies. Her comments on the book and her support and encouragement throughout the writing of it are greatly appreciated.

During the writing of the book we have also benefited from discussions, friendship, advice, encouragement, insightful suggestions, and constructive criticism from Martin Whyte, Michelle Lamont, Eric Fong, Liah Greenfeld, Michael Biggs, Ellen Judd, Jieyu Liu, Rachel Murphy, Man Yee Kwan, Cecilia Menjívar, Gilbert C. Gee, Brenda S. A. Yeoh, Wei-jun Jean Yeung and Jeffrey G. Reitz. The research on which this book is based has been presented at Oxford University, the School of Oriental and African Studies at the University of London, and the Centre for Gender Studies at Cambridge University. Some of the findings were also presented at conferences organized by the Gender Research Centre (Gender and Migration: Change and Challenges International Conference, December 10–11, 2013); the Department of Sociology (Migration and Identity: Perspectives from Asia, Europe and North America, March 6–7, 2015); and the Pearl River Delta Social Research Centre (Labor, Mobility and Development in the PRD and Beyond, June 6–7, 2015) at the Chinese University of Hong Kong; as well as at the Eighth Global Social Sciences Conference: Trans-disciplinary Approaches to Global Social Sciences, December 11–12, 2014, at Hong Kong Baptist University. We thank the audiences at these conferences for their constructive comments and suggestions.

We have been very lucky to have the opportunity to work with the executive editor of the University of California Press, Naomi Schneider, who is intelligent, efficient, kind, and supportive. We thank the competent and helpful Ally Power, Kate Warne, and Will Vincent at the press for their prompt responses to our questions during the publication process. We also thank Thomas Frick for his meticulous copy-editing help. We are grateful for the constructive comments and insights of two anonymous reviewers enlisted by the press. Their careful reading of the book and constructive criticism helped us to improve our writing and strengthen our central arguments.

The research for this book was supported by a grant from the Hong Kong Research Grant Council for work on "Masculinities in transition: Comparing gender identity construction among male migrant workers in the manufacturing, service, and construction sectors in South China." During the writing of the book Susanne was also supported by a Fulbright–RGC Hong Kong Senior Research Scholar Award. We also thank the Department of Sociology at Harvard University for providing Susanne with a visiting scholarship, during which part of the book was completed. Susanne's colleagues in the Sociology Department and Gender Research Centre at the Chinese University of Hong Kong have supported her on her academic journey and in her continual efforts to balance work with family life. Yinni would like to express her appreciation to her colleagues at the Department of Sociology, Hong Kong Baptist University, for their support and friendship.

Our heartfelt appreciation goes also to our families. Roman has been a rock for Susanne during their time together. It was at his insistence that she applied for the Fulbright–RGC Research Award, which enabled her to spend four months in the US focusing on the book. His promise to take good care of their two children, Jan and Antonin, while she was away helped to give her peace of mind so that she could concentrate on writing. Jan and Antonin would probably not understand the arguments of this book at the moment, but they certainly understand how it feels to be separated from one's parents; their father spent nine years working as a migrant father. Perhaps one day, when they have grown up, they will appreciate the efforts of migrants to make family work. Susanne's parents have given her immeasurable support, which has enabled her to juggle family responsibilities with work for the last twelve years. Their love and their own stories of migration and family separation were her original and most important motivation for writing this book. Yinni has been a migrant for more than seventeen years; she started her migration journey as a student in Beijing and Hong Kong, and then became a migrant worker in Hong Kong. Having been a migrant daughter for such a long time, Yinni feels indebted to her parents in Hunan, who always supported her decision to pursue an academic career. Their unconditional love, continuous encouragement, moral support, and practical help are what have kept Yinni going and enabled her to overcome all kinds of problems and difficulties during her migration journey.

Finally, we dedicate this book to all the migrants, and their families, who have worked so hard to overcome the odds and sustain familyhood across multiple locations.

CHAPTER I

Introduction

Migration, Family, and Masculinity in Postsocialist China

> The traditional Chinese economy and society were no more or less dependent upon the successful operation of the Confucian family system than vice versa. The family, the economy, and the society were, as we have seen, one system. That system was patriarchy.
>
> —Judith Stacey, *Patriarchy and Socialist Revolution in China*

We met Xie, a twenty-year-old male waiter at a newly built three-star hotel in Dongguang, an industrialized economic zone in South China, in December 2013. A tall, fair, and timid young man, native of Chong Qing, Xie told us that he had left his rural home at the age of fourteen because he was kicked out of school as a result of leading a gang fight. Xie used to be one of the millions of "left-behind children" in rural China. His parents left him in the care of his paternal grandmother when he was just three years old to *dagong* (work for others)—a term peasant workers used to describe their predicament as migrant workers in cities. They did not return for six years. When he missed his parents and asked why they did not return, his grandmother would point at a newly built house and tell him that this was concrete evidence of their love for him. The house was built for his future marriage using remittances from his parents. Xie's parents had high hopes for him. They hoped he would use the money they earned from *dagong* to attend university or at least to learn a skilled trade. Instead, Xie has changed jobs more than ten times in the six years since he began his *dagong* life. His next-to-last job was as a male sex worker in a glamorous five-star hotel in Yunnan province; this ended fairly uneventfully when he was infected with sexually transmitted diseases and forced to return to his parents, who were working in Dongguang at the time. When we spoke to him Xie was living with his parents in a rented apartment in one of the "villages in cities" (*chengzhongcun*)[1] not far from where he works. His grandmother still lived in the rural village, but he and his parents were saving to buy a flat in a town near to their rural village. He told us that he knew nothing about farming and could not imagine living the life of a peasant. He was not even planning to return to the village for the Spring Festival. Instead, he and his parents would celebrate it in Dongguang. Xie used to live with his girlfriend, whom his parents had approved to be his marital partner, but they split up when she found out about his sex work. Xie was fond of this girl because she washed all his clothes, cooked for him, and was frugal with money, which made her "virtuous wife" material, like his mother. Unlike his parents, Xie vowed that he would never leave his children behind and go out to *dagong*. Instead, he wanted to get married, raise children, and live happily with his family. Xie thought that he needed a successful career to make this dream come true. When we met him, this seemed only a distant possibility; as a waiter he earned a meager eighteen hundred yuan per month and spent it freely, most of it on visits to massage parlors, gambling, drinking with friends, and occasional consumption of soft drugs in the nearby karaoke bars. He did not seem to worry about his future; his parents had already built a house for him, they were saving for a down payment on a flat in the town, and they planned to send him to learn a skill after the Spring Festival.

Yao is a forty-five-year-old security guard from Hunan. He left his rural home for *dagong* in the cities of South China in 1989. When Yao left, his only child was nine years old. During the first five years of *dagong* life, his wife stayed behind to look after their son. She joined him in 2004 because he became sick and was not able to earn enough money for the family. When we met Yao in 2013, the first thing he told us was that he felt terribly guilty towards his parents, because he had not been home for the Spring Festival for eleven years. The second thing was that he felt sorry that his child had grown into adulthood without

---

1. Villages in cities are sometimes referred to as urban villages. These are enclaves and housing located both on the outskirts and in downtown areas of major migrant-receiving cities such as Beijing, Guangzhou, and Shenzhen in China. Rural-to-urban migrants are the major residents of villages in cities. Although living conditions in these villages are typically overcrowded and unsatisfactory, they provide some form of affordable housing for the millions of rural-to-urban migrants.

parental support. Yao's only consolation was that he counted himself a caring husband—while rural men seldom do domestic chores, Yao washed his wife's clothes, cooked for her, cleaned the small rented apartment that they shared, shopped for food, made the bed, and changed the linens. Yao did all these chores despite teasing from his fellow Hunanese. Yao's wife was the one who made all the important decisions for the family, a pattern departing remarkably from the tradition of male dominance and female subordination prescribed by Confucian teachings about conjugal power in China. Yao and his wife are also unconventional in that she had earned nearly twice as much as him as a factory worker at the time of our interview.

In the 1930s Chinese sociologist Fei Xiaotong saw "leaving the land but not the village" (*litu bu lixiang*), allowing China's rural peasants to combine small-scale industrial and agricultural production, as a viable strategy for addressing the agrarian crisis which, according to Stacey (1983), threatened the survival and legitimacy of the peasant patriarchy. Six decades later events in rural China had developed in exactly the direction that Fei wanted to prevent: since the 1980s rural China has experienced arguably the largest exodus in its history. According to the 2010 census, a staggering 220 million peasants have left their rural homes in search of better economic opportunities in the country's glittering new urban centers. What started as a trickle of individual migrants—mostly married rural men traveling to do temporary or seasonal work to supplement their income from agricultural production—has become a way of life for most peasants and their children: men and women, single and married, understand going out to *dagong* in cities as "the way things are," not something they have a choice about. This mass exodus has prompted concerned sociologists, journalists, and policy makers to develop terms such as "left-behind children" (*liushou ertong*), "hollow village," (*kongxincun*) and "lone-person village" (*yigeren de cunzhuang*) to describe villages inhabited only by young children and their elderly grandparents, and increasingly only the grandparents.

The image of the lone elderly peasant sitting in front of a newly built two-story brick house could not be further from the cultural ideal of the large, extended Chinese family, consisting of at least three generations—the patriarch and his wife, his married sons and their wives, and their grandchildren (Hsu, 1971). Although previous studies have suggested that the large joint family was an ideal rather than the norm throughout most of China's history, families consisting of three generations used to be common, accounting for around half of both urban and rural households (Unger, 1993; Harrell, 1993). Even after a family division (*fenjia*), linked households sometimes developed into "networked families" (*wangluo jiating*) (Unger, 1993) or "aggregate families" (Croll, 1994) to fulfill the traditional functions of caring for the elderly and the young. The massive migration of the young and able-bodied from rural China to urban areas represents an unprecedented crisis for families in rural China, because now nobody—including the senior leaders of the postsocialist state—can be certain that the elderly population in the countryside will have anything to fall back on, or that the young will be adequately nurtured.

Rural migration to urban areas not only makes fulfillment of the family's time-honored role as caretaker for the young and old an unprecedented challenge for the peasant family, it also shatters the foundation of the peasant patriarchy—the advantage and control men have over women, derived from the exclusion of women as full members of their natal families before marriage and their confinement to the domestic realm after marriage. Parents traditionally favored sons over daughters, because sons were the successors to the family name, lineage, and bloodline and were expected to support their parents in old age. Parents invested more in sons than daughters in the terms of education, housing, and land, because sons were a form of old-age security, while daughters were viewed as only temporary members of the household on whom the parents could not count. When a daughter married she had to move to live with or near her husband's family and transfer her allegiance to them, a practice variously termed "patrilocal residence," "patrilocality," or "virilocal marriage." The saying that describes a married daughter as "water splashing out," the labeling of daughters as "a loss" (*peibenhuo*), and the custom of having the mother's face look toward the outward door when giving birth to daughters all symbolized the outsider status of a Chinese daughter in her natal family. It is also no coincidence that the Chinese character for "marry" (*jia* 嫁) represents a female figure outside the family. The one-child policy has begun to change daughters' second-class status in the family. By making it legitimate for only-child daughters to live with or close to their parents after marriage, this policy makes them available to provide old-age care and changes the cultural dynamics and expectations that devalue women (Unger, 1993). Although statistical evidence suggests that patrilocal residence is still the norm in rural areas (Judd, 1994; Harrell, 1993), there are also signs that rural-to-urban migration may be one mechanism behind the gradual change in the practice of patrilocality. Rural-to-urban migration dramatically weakens parental control and strengthens the conjugal bond when a couple migrate together; it may thus increase the bargaining power of female migrant workers negotiating to live near their own rather than their husband's family after marriage.

Men's dominance over women in Chinese society was traditionally based on a rigid system of sex segregation that reserved the public realm for men, secluding and confining women to the domestic sphere (Mann, 2011). The Chinese character for "wife" graphically depicts her as a domestic figure (*neiren*): it represents a female figure with a broom(婦). Although the Communist revolution encouraged women's participation in production, thus dramatically reducing the "outside/inside" segregation of the sexes, to date none of the reforms have fundamentally altered the fact that the domestic sphere is women's responsibility (Croll, 1983; Judd, 1994; Yan, 2003). Rural-to-urban migration may yet change this dynamic. While rural men consider the idea that they would do domestic chores laughable (Judd, 1994), peasant men in urban centers, such as Yao, have no choice but to negotiate responsibility for domestic chores. This is particularly true for peasant men in migrant couples (men who migrate to the city with their spouse) and migrant families (peasant men who migrate to the city with their wife and children). Away from the village these families often do not have access to extended family support for child care, and as they are typically in the city's lowest social stratum they are unable to afford paid child care. The financial pressures on migrant families with children are particularly testing: migrants are denied full citizenship in the city they live in, and their children are denied access to public education (Goodburn, 2009). This makes paid employment for the wife an economic necessity, which in turn necessitates conjugal renegotiation of responsibility for domestic chores and child care, so that husband and wife can combine work and family responsibilities. The impact of this renegotiation of the centuries-old "outside/inside" division of roles between peasant men and women, and the ways in which it may transform Chinese patriarchy, are extremely interesting issues.

Despite the potentially massive impact of rural-to-urban migration on the Chinese family, there has been little systematic research in this area. Previous studies of rural-to-urban migration focused on its economic, political, and health impacts. When effects on the family were explored, the focus was on quantifiable outcomes, such as family wealth, child health, and the well-being of the elderly; internal family negotiation processes were left largely unexamined. The few studies to look at the interpersonal dynamics and emotionality of family negotiations resulting from rural-to-urban migration mostly did so from the standpoint of women, either as migrant workers or left-behind wives (Gaetano and Jacka, 2004; Jacka, 2006, 2012). The voices and subjective experiences of peasant men are curiously absent from the academic record. This absence coincides with a similar gap in literature on Western migration, and constitutes an important lacuna in our understanding of how the colossal migration from rural to urban China may have transformed that pillar of Chinese society, the patriarchal family system. The neglect of Chinese peasant men's voices may perhaps stem from the view that peasant men are the de facto beneficiaries of patriarchy, and hence their experiences are unproblematic and do not warrant extensive investigation. However, gender is not a fixed, individual attribute; gender is relational. Inequalities between the sexes originated in interactions between men and women, and the intersection between interactional and institutional contexts. We would be hard pressed to develop a full understanding of exactly how the Chinese patriarchal family is produced, reproduced, challenged, and transformed by migration without considering the subjective experience and agency of men. Furthermore, men are not a homogenous group. Inequalities between men, and how these have shaped patriarchy, has become a burgeoning area of study in the West under the banner of masculinity research (Connell, 1987), but this theoretical perspective has seldom been employed to understand the experiences of male peasant workers in urban China.

Most studies of the Chinese family have focused on the "structural principles" of the "corporate family," thus leaving issues of intimacy, emotionality, and individual agency largely unaccounted for (Yan, 2003). Judd (1994) has also suggested that previous studies had prioritized interhousehold and external dynamics over intrahousehold processes. It is the Chinese family's public manifestation, including economic, political, and juridical aspects, that has attracted the attention of scholars. In reviewing Stacey's acclaimed book *Patriarchy and Socialist Revolution in China*, Watson (1985: 62) laments that "for a book about the family, there is not much here about the internal dynamics of domestic life." The marginalization in academic literature of the internal, domestic life of the Chinese family has gone hand-in-hand with an almost total absence of interest in conjugality. When scholars have considered the domestic dynamics of Chinese family life, the spotlight has been fixed firmly on intergenerational relationships, for instance the father-son bond (Hsu, 1971), the mother-child bond (Wolf, 1972; Evans, 2008), or the antagonism between mothers-in-law and daughters-in-law (Wolf, 1968; Gallin, 1994). The absence of the conjugal dimension may be related to the fact that in the Confucian discourse of the Chinese patriarchal family, "the husband-wife relationship is strictly held to be supplementary and subordinate to the parents-son relationship" (Hsu, 1971: 57), although scholars have suggested that variations in custom and class practice may have resulted in much stronger bonds between husband and wife than the official model permitted (Hsu, 1971; Stacey, 1983). The omission of conjugality from the literature on the Chinese family is even less justifiable today, given that the Communist state has dramatically redefined the family as a "form of joint life of two sexes united in marriage" (Stacey, 1983: 4). Yan (2003: 86) has argued that "the triumph of conjugal power" was one of the key changes to the Chinese family and could not be overlooked. Whether Yan (2003) overstated the case is debatable; nevertheless he pointed out the increasingly central role of conjugal dynamics in Chinese family life, even in rural families.

In summary, previous studies of migration, family, and gender in China have overlooked three issues: they have prioritized outcome over process and structural principles over emotionality; men's voices and subjective experience are missing from the academic literature; and conjugality has been marginalized. This book departs from previous research in three important respects in order to address these gaps. First, it examines the impact of rural-to-urban migration on family dynamics and intrafamily negotiation processes rather than looking at quantifiable outcomes, as previous studies have done. Second, it specifically considers the emotional dimension of intergenerational dynamics and devotes considerable space to discussing individual agency in conjugal negotiations. Third, it looks at the voices and subjective experiences of male migrant workers, and uses peasant men's experiences and narratives to analyze how migration has transformed the family.

MIGRATION RESEARCH IN CHINA: THE FAMILY AND GENDER GAPS

Since the Communist Party came to power in 1949 it has relied predominantly on the household registration system (*hukou*) as a means of restricting the geographical mobility of its population. Under the *hukou* system, which assigned every Chinese citizen a particular place of residence, rural residents were not allowed to migrate to cities, and urban residents were prohibited from moving between cities. In the late 1970s and 1980s, following the gradual removal of barriers to rural-to-urban migration, post-Mao China probably witnessed the largest human migration in history (Peng, 2011). The 2010 census in China estimated that around 260 million Chinese people were living away from the place where their *hukou* (household registration) was recorded. This colossal population of migrants included about 220 million people migrating from rural to urban areas (National Bureau of Statistics of China, 2011a), the so-called floating population. Migration from rural to urban areas has not only had a tremendous impact on China's economic development, urbanization, and rural development, it has also shaped millions of rural families. Some scholars have estimated that around half of China's rural population of more than six hundred million live in households with at least one migrant worker (Démurger and Xu, 2011). Because of the overlapping constraints of the *hukou* system and rural land tenure arrangements, the vast majority of rural-to-urban migrants are "circular migrants," who maintain close ties with their family in the source community throughout the process of migration (Fan, 2008). However, there are increasing numbers of permanent migrants (Hu, Xu, and Chen, 2011) and returned migrants (Gao and Jia, 2007). Regardless of type, rural-to-urban migration entails migrants physically leaving their family; it creates split households and forces family affairs to be transacted across multiple geographical locations. This generates new opportunities and tensions, allowing family members to renegotiate their familial roles and obligations, as well as potentially affecting the distribution of power and resources and posing a new challenge to the maintenance of emotional bonds, intimacy, and loyalty between family members.

A search for publications including the words "migration" and "China" via Google Scholar suggests that the vast majority of existing research has focused on the impact of migration on economic development, work conditions and labor resistance, urbanization, access to health care, and HIV/AIDS. Studies examining the impact of migration on family life are in a minority. The lack of research in this area stands in sharp contrast to the central role the family plays in Chinese society and the importance of the family system as a mechanism for maintaining the Chinese patriarchy. There are three possible explanations for the relative lack of research on migration and the family. First, the image of the typical rural-to-urban migrant is of a young, single worker, epitomized in the phrases *dagongmei* (factory girl) (Chang, 2008) and *dagongzai* (factory boy). Although this image may have represented the earliest cohort of female migrant workers who left the countryside to work in the export-driven processing zones in South China (see for example Lee, 1998), it was not valid for the earliest cohort of male migrant workers, let alone the majority of the floating population thirty years after the unleashing of this prodigious migration. Several studies have shown that more male migrant workers were married than single (Choi and Du, 2011). According to the 2000 census, around 73 percent of those classified as the floating population were married (Wong, Li, and Song, 2007). The misconception that migrants tend to be single may result in the view that migration is a temporary stage in an individual's life cycle, that physical separation from family in the source community is a short-term experience, and that migration has only a brief, limited impact on family life. Recent statistics have showed that for many rural-to-urban migrants, migration is not a transitional experience; it begins in early adulthood and extends well into their late fifties (Loyalka, 2012; National Bureau of Statistics of the People's Republic of China, 2013). In addition, although the majority of rural-to-urban migrants may be circulators, the duration of their physical separation from their family is anything but short. Because China is such a geographically vast country, traveling between the source community and the destination community may take days and cost migrants a hefty proportion of their often meager income. Coupled with the difficulty of obtaining leave from work in some sectors, these factors mean that migrants' temporary separation from the family left behind may be measured in years rather than months. Given the number of lifelong circulators, who are often forced into separation from their family for extended periods of time, the challenges that China's internal migration poses to family life are far from negligible.

Second, while the majority of the earliest cohort of rural migrants was men, the percentage of female migrants has increased rapidly over the last thirty years. The 2000 census showed that women accounted for 49.6 percent of the floating population (Cai, 2003). More importantly, the nature of female migration has changed over the years. The 1990 census showed that the majority of male migrants migrated for work reasons (60 percent), whereas most women migrated for family reasons (56 percent). Women migrants were also more likely to return to their community of origin because of family and caring responsibilities (Zhu, 2005). In summary, the majority of the earliest cohorts of female migrants in China were either dependents of migrants or their migration trajectory was truncated by family responsibilities. This is consistent with the traditional Chinese gender norm that anchors femininity in wifehood and motherhood (Mann, 2011). However, there is evidence that an increasing number of female migrant workers prioritize work over family life, enjoying the newfound independence and power their city income has brought them and contemplating settling permanently in the city (Yan, 2008; Zhu and Chen, 2010; Chang, 2008). The question of how this transformation of the female experience of migration, and women's attitudes toward migration, will affect the Chinese patriarchy and shape conjugal relationships remains to be answered.

Third, while it is true that early cohorts of rural-to-urban migrants tended to be circulators and were therefore able to maintain close relationships with their family in their community of origin, this may no longer be true; an increasing number of temporary migrants are seeking permanent settlement opportunities in the city. The effect this has on how left-behind elderly parents are cared for may shake the foundations of the Chinese family system and undermine the ethos of filial piety.

Finally, the stereotype of rural-to-urban migrants as individuals rather than as part of a larger household has distracted scholars from the investigation of postmigration intrahousehold dynamics. New evidence has suggested that the pattern of rural-to-urban migration has gradually shifted; whereas male married migrants used to leave their children, wife, and elderly parents behind, nowadays migration tends to involve couples or even the whole nuclear family. Fan (2008) showed that couple and family migration has increased. The rapid expansion of "villages in cities" in urban China provides further evidence of the changing pattern of rural-to-urban migration; single workers living in dormitories are giving way to migrant families settling on the margins of affluent urban communities.

These changes raise questions about how the internal dynamics of family life have been affected by migration, yet most of the limited number of studies of migration and family in China have focused on the economic consequences (Qin, 2010). In particular, researchers have explored how migrants' remittances to their families may ameliorate rural poverty (Taylor, Rozelle, and de Brauw, 2003; Du, Park, and Wang, 2005; Huang and Zhan, 2008; De Brauw and Rozelle, 2008). More recently, other studies have begun to investigate the impact of rural-to-urban migration on the well-being of the so-called "left-behind children" (Zhou et al., 2005; Liang, Guo, and Duan, 2008; Liu, Li, and Ge, 2009; Chen et al., 2009; Gao et al., 2010; Fan et al., 2010; Jia and Tian, 2010; Qin and Albin, 2010; Ye and Pan, 2011; Lee, 2011; Lu, 2012; Wen and Lin, 2012; Zhou, Murphy, and Tao, 2014; Murphy, 2014; Wu, 2014;

Wu, Tsang, and Ming, 2014). A smaller body of research has examined the impact of migration on elderly care (Pang, de Brauw, and Rozelle, 2004; Guo, Aranda, and Silverstein, 2009; Giles, Wang, and Zhao, 2010; Chang, Dong, and MacPhail, 2011; He and Ye, 2014). Research on how migration shapes conjugal dynamics is conspicuously lacking (Jacka, 2012), although a few articles have addressed issues related to left-behind wives (Xiang, 2007; Jacka, 2012).

Gender is also a lacuna in research into migration and the family. A review of literature showed that migration studies in China touching on the issue of gender can be divided into two categories. Research in the first category compares the differences between male and female migrants and explains them in terms of macrostructural factors such as gender norm socialization (see Choi and Du, 2011, for a review); the second category focuses on the particular experiences of female migrants (Lee, 1998; Pun, 2005b; Yan, 2008; Gaetano and Jacka, 2004; Zhang, 2014; Chiang, Hannum, and Kao, 2015). Although these studies have enriched our understanding of the dynamic interaction between gender and migration, they have left the particular experiences of male migrant workers unexplored. This omission is especially unfortunate, because while female migrant workers may be doubly marginalized in cities, male migrant workers often have to cope with the discrepancy between their dominance in rural China and their marginalization in cities. The household-based agrarian economy, patrilineal inheritance, and patrilocal postmarriage residence backed by Confucian ideology are the foundations of Chinese patriarchy (Zuo, 2009). Although there have been changes in China as a result of economic reform and modernization, scholars argue that the overall structure of the Chinese patriarchy, specifically the dual backbone of patrilineal inheritance combined with patrilocal residence, remained largely intact until the mid-1990s (Stacey, 1983; Judd 1994; Hershatter, 2004). Rural men, especially married rural men, largely hold the authority, control the distribution of resources, and dominate the economic activities of the patrilineal family; they are held responsible for the performance and success of their family. Rural men are expected to build a house, take a wife, and become head of a household. Migration to cities is often a way of meeting these expectations. Economic achievement therefore has dual significance for male rural migrants: it is a means of improving the material conditions of their family and the ultimate barometer of their manhood. The reality, however, stands in sharp contrast to their expectations. Contemporary China is characterized by inequalities embodied in the structure of work units (*danwei*) (Lin and Bian, 1991) and household registration (the *hukou* system); these systems exclude migrant workers from the social security program (Solinger, 1999), better-paid jobs (Cai and Wang, 2008), urban housing market (Song, Zenou, and Ding, 2008), and public services such as education and health care (Goodburn, 2014), relegating them to the status of second-class citizens in cities (Wu and Treiman, 2007). Excluded and marginalized, rural-to-urban male migrants are nonetheless judged according to the ideal of dominant manhood that prevails in popular discourse in the cities. This hegemonic discourse of masculinity stresses male virility, wealth, and entrepreneurship (Lu, 2000; Zhang, 2007; Uretsky, 2008). In addition to these discrepancies, rural-to-urban migration may fundamentally alter the gender and power dynamics of the Chinese family system, rendering the continued dominance of men problematic.

MIGRATION AND GENDER IN THE WEST: THE ABSENCE OF MALE VOICES AND SUBJECTIVE EXPERIENCE

Over the past three decades many scholars, particularly feminist ethnographers, have worked to "bring gender from the periphery to the core of migration studies" (Mahler and Pessar, 2006: 27). This body of research has drawn attention to the central role gender plays in decisions about migration, the process and outcome of settlement in the host society, and decisions about return (Hondagneu-Sotelo, 1994; Phizacklea, 2003; Hagan, 1998; Boyd, 1989; Ong, 1987; Constable, 1997; Hondagneu-Sotelo, 2001; Choi and Du, 2011; Lan, 2006; Flippen and Parrado, 2015). However, despite the insistence on the importance of gender in migration research, male migrants' voices and accounts of men's subjective experience has remained largely abstract, shadowy, or confined in domains traditionally considered as masculine. This is especially true of studies in developing countries, where the disadvantages of women are still considered the major challenge to gender research. In 1984, *International Migration Review* published a special issue entitled "Women in Migration" to counter the "male bias" in early migration research that portrayed the typical migrant as a young male and neglected the particular experiences of women migrants, or represented them in terms of the stereotype of "passive dependents" in migration research and policy (Morokvasic, 1984). This special issue presented a wide array of evidence for the centrality of women in patterns of internal and international migration, and the variable impact of migration on gender relationships in both the sending and receiving communities. Ten years later, *International Migration Review* published a follow-up special issue entitled "A Glass Half Full? Gender in Migration Studies." While praising the 1984 publication for "bringing female migration out of the shadows" (Donato et al., 2006: 4), this new special issue highlighted the importance of a relational understanding of gender in migration research. By viewing migration as a gendered process, editors of this special issue drew distinctions between male-centered, female-centered and gender-blind gender analysis. A gender analysis of migration recognizes men and women as subjects of inquiry and also conceptualizes gender as more than a simple dichotomous variable. In a gender analysis of migration, gender, according to the editors of this special issue, is relational, contextualized, and multiscalar.

A detailed look at the burgeoning literature on gender and migration covered in this special issue and related works shows that, despite the emphasis on gender as a relational construct, most research still relies predominantly on the views of female respondents. Men are nearly always included in large-sample quantitative research, such as studies of ethnic enclaves, segmented assimilation, and postmigration incorporation. However, the focus of quantitative studies very rarely extends beyond a simple comparison of male and female differences, and the explanation for any gender differences is usually speculative. Most qualitative research on gender and migration relies mainly on data provided by female respondents. With the notable exceptions of work by Lin (2013), Hoang and Yeoh (2011, 2012), Hoang, Yeoh, and Wattie (2012), Cheng, Yeoh, and Zhang (2015), Dreby (2010), Hondagneu-Sotelo (2014), and Schmalzbauer (2015), men in migrant families usually appear in the narratives of their wives, mothers, and sisters. Their voices are seldom heard firsthand, and their subjective experience is represented by their female family members. When the subjective experience of men is placed center stage in migration research, the focus is usually on their work life (Lin, 2013; Baey and Yeoh, 2015) or on deviant behaviors such as men's alcohol consumption, drug and gambling addiction, violence perpetration, role in HIV/AIDS transmission, and criminal engagement (Walter, Bourgois, and Loinaz, 2004; Bourgois, 1996a; Cohen, 2006; Lewis, 2014).

Ordinary, heterosexual migrant men's voices and subjective experience are largely absent from the gender and migration literature, with some recent exceptions. For example, Parreñas's study of Filipino transnational fathering (2008) suggested that migrant fathers were more willing to participate in housework than husbands in wife-away transnational families; migrant fathers' economic contribution gave them a secure sense of masculinity, while the inability of husbands in wife-away families to fulfill the role of breadwinner prompted them to refuse housework because it might reinforce their homemaker identity. Charsley's (2005) study of Pakistani men who immigrated to Britain through marriage argued that although most men faced precarious economic conditions and domestic pressure, there were two distinct strategies for coping with the crisis of masculinity that this implied: some men unleashed their frustration through "violence, desertion, or taking a second wife" (p. 85), while other men accepted the situation and dealt with their crisis of masculinity by fulfilling "the role of a good son" (p. 100). Lin (2014) analyzed how rural-to-urban migrants in China reworked their role as filial sons after migration. Other studies have argued that migrant men's higher earning power may allow them to maintain a high status in their community of origin and consolidate their domestic authority (Osella and Osella, 2000; Walter, Bourgois, and Loinaz, 2004; Broughton, 2008). These and other studies (see for example Castañeda and Buck, 2011; Smith, 2006; Menjívar, 2000; Boehm, 2012) suggest that family life is central to the understanding and expression of migrant masculinity.

MASCULINITY: CONSTRUCTED, NEGOTIATED, AND CONTEXTUALIZED

A folk interpretation of masculinity views it as the "psychological essence" of manhood, whereas sex role theory conceives masculinity as an aspect of identity that is acquired during early childhood socialization. Conceiving masculinity as an intrinsic aspect of being a man rules out questions about the social processes by which it is constructed, and which are in turn legitimized by it. On the other hand, viewing masculinity as a product of early childhood socialization neglects questions related to change, power, and structure (Goffman, 1977; West and Zimmerman, 1987). Connell (1993) used both reasons to advocate placing masculinity research in the framework of "the political sociology of men in gender relations" (p. 601). In a series of thought-provoking studies, Connell (1987, 1993, 1998, 2003) argued that there exists in most societies a culturally normative ideal of manhood. Borrowing from Gramsci's notion of "ideological hegemony," Connell asserted that this hegemonic masculinity reflects, makes "natural" and legitimizes social arrangements that privilege the dominant group in society (e.g. white, middle-class, heterosexual men in Western capitalist societies) (see also Kimmel, 2005). Although hegemonic masculinity is the dominant gender ideology and has a correspondingly strong influence on the practice of manhood, men who are subordinated and marginalized because of their class, ethnicity, migration status, or sexual orientation are forced to confront the discrepancy between cultural ideals and their structural locations. Their lower social status also forces them to mobilize other resources and construct alternative discourses of manhood (Bourgois, 1996b; Cruz, 2000; Nardi, 2000; Mutchler, 2000; Cohn and Enloe, 2003).

In this framework masculinity is understood both as a normative ideal of manhood at the ideological and discursive level, and in terms of personal practice that is closely linked with the institutions of the state, the workplace and labor market, and the family. Masculinity thus must be located in the social stratification mechanisms that produce inequality between men and women and between groups of men (Donaldson, 1993; Connell and Messerschmidt, 2005). It is a construction that is historically and culturally specific (Baron, 2006; Heron, 2006; McCoyer, 2006). Conceiving masculinity in these terms means that a particular concept of masculinity and its expression can be analyzed within a specific historical and cultural context, and in terms of four dimensions: personal, interpersonal, institutional, and cultural (Lusher and Robins, 2009). Personal factors may include an individual's gender-role beliefs; interpersonal factors may include the pattern of interactions in close relationships, for example between migrant men and their aging parents or their spouse and left-behind children; institutional factors may include structural inequalities related to rural or urban residency, and workplace practices that make it challenging to combine paid employment and parenthood in an urban setting without extended family support or the financial resources to access paid child care; cultural factors include the different dominant discourses of ideal manhood and family obligations in rural communities and urban society, and how the disjunction between the two affects men.

Connell (1992) put it very well: "The study of men is as vital for gender analysis as the study of ruling classes and elites is for class analysis" (p. 736). It has been argued that women are not born, but become women (de Beauvoir, 1952), and that male identity has been problematized and is no longer taken for granted (Kimmel, Hearn, and Connell, 2005). In our case, making masculinity visible helps us question the origins, structures, and dynamics of inequalities between men and women within the family, and inequalities between groups of men in society (Connell,

1987; Kimmel and Messner, 2010). It also sheds light on the strategies men use to "do gender" (West and Zimmerman, 1987) and construct a positive sense of self when confronted by challenges and crises generated by migration.

THE CITIES AND THE RURAL MALE MIGRANTS

Three research sites were used in this study: Dongguan, Shenzhen, and Guangzhou, all in South China. Dongguan is host to more than fifteen thousand foreign companies specializing in electronics and the IT industry, textiles and clothing, furniture, toys, and chemical products. The second author of this book conducted ethnographic fieldwork at factories in Dongguan between 2007 and 2009 and is very familiar with the dynamics of its migrant population and the local settings. It was therefore the ideal place for us to recruit male migrants working in the manufacturing sector. Shenzhen was chosen as our second field site in order to recruit male migrants working in service industries. The service industry has become the second-largest industrial sector, absorbing 35 percent of migrant workers in Shenzhen in 2010.[2] Guangzhou, the capital of Guangdong province, is one of the largest cities in South China and had a population of 12.92 million in 2013. Rapid modernization means that when we conducted our field research there were numerous infrastructure and construction projects in operation, most of which rely on migrant workers. It was therefore an appropriate site for the recruitment of male migrants working in the construction sector. In view of the fact that age and marital status may affect the meaning and expression of masculinity (Du, 2011), we limited our sample to men between eighteen and sixty years of age.

Between 2012 and 2015, our research team visited six "villages in cities" in Shenzhen, Dongguan, and Guangzhou in the course of fifteen field trips. During each field trip, we observed the daily lives of migrant workers, had conversations with hotel and restaurant owners, street peddlers, truck drivers, taxi drivers, motor-taxi drivers, beauticians, cleaners, waiters, and migrant parents picking up children after school. We also conducted in-depth interviews with 192 migrant men and 74 migrant women. These interviews included eleven couple interviews. In

2. "The report of living status of the new generation of migrant workers in Shenzhen." Shenzhen Trade Union, 2010, http://acftu.people.com.cn/GB/67583/12155296 .html

this book, we drew mainly on the interviews with the 192 men, although we also cross-checked the validity of their accounts with the interviews with women. In particular, the eleven couple interviews were analyzed to help us understand conjugal dynamics as discussed in chapters 4 and 5.

The mean age of our 191 male respondents (one male respondent finished the in-depth interview but did not complete the questionnaire) was thirty-six years. The mean age at which they began *dagong* life in the cities was twenty-three years. One hundred thirty-seven of our respondents were married (71 percent), two cohabited with a partner, two were widowed, four were divorced, and forty-six were single. One hundred thirty-four of our respondents had children. Slightly more than half of our respondents (111) were individual migrants, fifty-one had migrated as part of a couple, and another thirty had been part of a family migration. In terms of occupational distributions, we made sure that our sample covered the major occupations of male rural-to-urban migrants. Our respondents included thirteen migrant workers who had succeeded in finding a white-collar role, nineteen men working in the hotel and catering sector, most as cooks or waiters, forty-four construction workers, forty-seven taxi drivers, nineteen factory workers, thirty-six security guards, and fourteen men in various economic roles such as grocery shop/restaurant/vegetable stall owners, unpaid family workers, hairdressers, sales clerks, cleaners, electricians, etc.

When we started our fieldwork we were concerned about the gender dynamic of women interviewing men. To minimize any interviewer gender effects we included five men in our team of ten trained interviewers. We also matched interviewers and respondents according to age: for example, we avoided having young female interviewers interviewing young male migrant workers. Young male migrant workers were either interviewed by male interviewers or by the two senior female interviewers in the research team, who approached them as an older aunt- or sister-figure to avoid embarrassment in discussion of intimate issues. Comparison of the interview data obtained by male and female interviewers did not reveal any systematic interviewer-related biases. Previous studies have suggested two conflicting gendered dynamics of interviews. On the one hand, same-gender identification is argued to be a precondition for successful interviews; on the other hand, some studies suggest that cross-gender discussion is easier for some topics. For example, men often find it easier to discuss pregnancy with a woman interviewer than with another man (Lee, 1997). In our interviews we observed both patterns; young male respondents seemed to be more forth-coming about entertainment, friendship, and male subculture with young male interviewers, while many male migrant workers were surprisingly willing to discuss conjugal dynamics and intergenerational emotional dynamics with our female interviewers. Quite a few male respondents told our female interviewers that they could never have discussed such issues with their friends, and that they greatly appreci-ated having the opportunity to talk about these more intimate and emotional issues. There is a cultural expectation that Chinese men will not express their emotions, yet five male respondents cried during the interviews as they were sharing stories about a sick wife, separation from girlfriends, and arguments with their spouse. It may be that rather than being a hindrance, having women interview men presents an opportunity; men often value aspects of the female world (e.g. its emo-tionality) that they are not supposed to share, and are generally excluded from.

THE ORGANIZATION OF THE BOOK

The book is composed of eight chapters. Following this introduction, chapter 2 provides a sketch of the *dagong* life of our respondents. It contextualizes their experiences within the broader contours of rural and urban inequalities, the state engineering of economic moderniza-tion, and the regulation of migration flows in postsocialist China. Chap-ter 3 tells the stories of how migrant men negotiate love and intimacy in cities and balance individual choices with parental influence. Chapter 4 looks at the issues of conjugal power negotiation resulting from and related to migration, the continuities in, as well as changes to, the tradi-tional pattern of male dominance within a marriage. Chapter 5 exam-ines how the novel context provided by rural-to-urban migration makes negotiation of housework an important issue for couples, and how migrant men developed a counterdiscourse of manhood to justify their increased participation in the domestic sphere. Chapter 6 explores the paradox of absentee fatherhood: while migration has allowed these fathers to fulfill their instrumental role of providing for their children, it has resulted in multifaceted emotional gaps. Chapter 7 examines how, as faraway sons, migrant men reconcile with their failure to serve their parents physically and financially, as expected by the teaching of filial piety in Chinese culture, and their efforts to reinterpret the obligation to care for elderly parents in emotional terms. Based on the findings of the preceding chapters, chapter 8 develops the concept of masculine compromise to account for changing gender practices and identity related to migration. It provides a feminist framework to analyze the ways in which migration transforms the family, and how migrant men interpret and respond to these transformations.

FIGURE 1. Entrance of a "village in the city" in Guangzhou
(photo by Susanne Y. P. Choi).

FIGURE 2. Living conditions in "villages in cities" are crowded, but they are nonetheless spaces where migrant workers can have a temporary home of their own (photo by Tang Chung Wang).

FIGURE 3. View of a "village in the city" in Shenzhen. "Villages in cities" are liminal spaces where traditional values and lingering poverty rub shoulders with modern aspirations (photo by Tang Chung Wang).

FIGURE 4. A migrant worker waits for business (removal services) (photo by Tang Chung Wang).

FIGURE 5. A group of migrant men working as motorbike/truck drivers take a break in the afternoon to catch up with their coethnics (photo by Tang Chung Wang).

FIGURE 6. Three young migrant workers, just arrived from their native home in Guizhou, ready to try their luck in the city (photo by Tang Chung Wang).

FIGURE 7. A migrant man selling candied fruit in the city. His wife stays in the village to look after their granddaughter (photo by Tang Chung Wang).

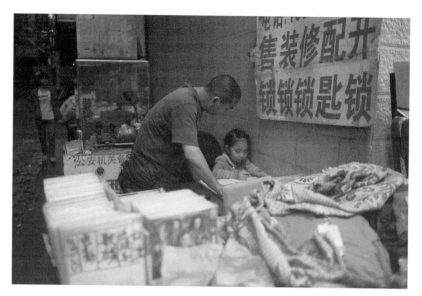

FIGURE 8. A migrant worker running a street stall teaches his daughter to do homework after school (photo by Tang Chung Wang).

FIGURE 9. A migrant father picks up his two children after school in a "village in the city" in Shenzhen (photo by Tang Chung Wang).

CHAPTER 2

Marginal Men and China's Grand Narratives

FENG: "FILLING OUR STOMACHS IS ENOUGH."

We met Feng, a forty-two-year-old renovation worker, in Shenzhen in early 2013. Wearing a brown nylon jacket and a pair of black trousers splashed with mud, Feng was fat, with a large beer belly, and had bright eyes. He felt a little bit uneasy at the beginning, but relaxed after lighting a cigarette and started to share his migration experiences with us.

Feng is from a poor village in rural Henan. He joined the army when he was nineteen years old and served for four years. In 1994, after being released from military service, he returned to his native village to take up a job in his village's forestry station; the job was arranged by the government as a reward for army service. The job did not bring him a stable income, however, since the salaries of all forestry station staff depended on the fines they collected from poor villagers. Feng stated that as a man of conscience and compassion, he could not accept that his salary came from the unreasonable fines extorted from poor villagers. His approach to the work was very passive, and consequently he took home a salary that was barely adequate to support his family.

Before Feng joined the army, he had been introduced to a girl in a nearby village. Feng's family is poverty-stricken and their dire economic conditions constrained both his choice of partner and the timing of his marriage. As Feng acknowledged, "I expected to find a better one [female partner]. However, my family was poor. I was worried that I might not be able to find a wife. So, I thought, 'Forget about it. Finding a wife is good enough.'" His impoverished family background also meant that he had to wait six years while he accumulated the resources necessary to marry his fiancée. One year after their marriage Feng's wife gave birth to their first son. Although the family was joyful about the arrival of a male heir, they were destitute. Feng recalled that, other than at the Spring Festival, his family barely had meat dishes on the table. Their income was so low that they needed credit even to buy salt. He could not afford milk or snacks for his son. Desperate, Feng believed that migration to the city was the only way he could save his family from poverty. In 1998 Feng migrated to Shenzhen for the first time. However, what awaited him in Shenzhen was not a good job but a horrible and humiliating experience.

As we will discuss later, between 1985 and 2003 the Chinese government used the temporary-residence certificate (*zanzhuzheng*) to regulate and limit the numbers of migrant workers in cities without urban *hukou*. This measure gave local governments the power to regulate the temporary population through the issuing of temporary-residence certificates, and the fines paid by migrant workers without these certificates became a source of revenue for them. After arriving in Shenzhen, Feng found a job as a street peddler selling steam buns, but he was arrested by the local police so quickly that he earned only few hundred yuan. Feng was sent to a labor camp in Shaoguan, a city in north Guangdong. Fifteen years after his arrest, Feng was still furious when he recalled the inhumane treatment he experienced in detention. He recalled that over thirty people were detained in a very small room without any toilet facilities. They had to huddle on one wide bed. Their food was putrid rice and salted turnip. Feng told the camp managers that he was a demobilized serviceman who had migrated to Shenzhen for employment. He explained that he had not applied for a temporary-residence certificate because he had been in Shenzhen only a few days and was not familiar with the rules. His explanation and pleas did not help secure his release. He was detained in the labor camp for five days and was released only after his friend paid the three hundred yuan fine. This experience was disheartening for Feng. As a demobilized serviceman and a Communist Party member, he found it hard to believe that the staff who mistreated him at the labor camp were also Communist Party members. As he stated, "At that time, the local government was corrupt. I seriously doubted those people arresting me were Communist Party members. I suspected that they were hooligans. How could Communist Party members do such abhorrent things?" Disillusioned, Feng returned to his village upon his release.

This unpleasant experience scared Feng. He stayed in the village and made his living by farming until 2002. During this period he and his wife had their second child, and family expenses increased. Feng embarked on his second migration attempt in 2002. He went to Weihai in Shangdong province and worked there as a security guard in a local public security bureau. He worked there for only one month because of the low salary (450 yuan per month) and long working hours (over twelve hours a day). In 2003 the central government abolished the temporary-residence certificates, and Feng migrated to Shenzhen for the second time, after hearing that local governments in the Pearl River Delta no longer arrested migrant workers without residence certificates. He joined a housing renovation team as a worker and earned sixty to seventy yuan per day. Feng admitted that his salary was not enough to support his whole family. As he explained, "If only one person migrates to take a job in the city, he or she may not make enough money [to support the family]. After deducting the rent and daily expenses [of the city worker], there will be very little money left. If a couple migrate together, they will make more money." Because Feng's salary depended on the number of orders his team received, it was not stable. His wife soon joined him. She found work in a labor-intensive factory in Shenzhen. Working eleven hours a day, she earned twenty-five to twenty-six hundred yuan per month in 2013. The couple worked long hours and lived an extremely frugal life so as to save enough money to build a house in their village and support their two left-behind children and elderly parents. To reduce their expenses, Feng and his wife did not visit their village between 2003 and 2006. Every year, they sent two thousand to three thousand yuan to Feng's parents, who helped to care for their left-behind children and paid for tuition, food, and other expenses. Although they were in their seventies, Feng's parents still made a living by farming and helped to tend Feng's land.

Feng had relatively low expectations for his work and life. He frankly admitted that other than raising his two children to maturity and caring for his elderly parents, he no longer had any goal for himself. Neither did he dream of a better life. He repeatedly told us, "Filling our stomachs is enough." Feng also did not think his children would be able to achieve any greater success. "Getting a job and earning enough money to fill their stomachs" was all Feng expected from his children. Feng realized that it would be hard for him to stay in the city permanently, as his income was low and unstable, while daily expenses in urban areas were already high and continued to soar. He concluded that returning to the village would be his only option, were he to lose his job. He believed that as long as he had the land, he could make a living by farming.

ZHANG: "SHORT OF THE BEST, BUT BETTER THAN THE WORST."

Zhang, a thirty-four-year-old security guard we met in Shenzhen in January 2013, was from rural Henan. Zhang migrated to Shenzhen for the first time in 1996. Being an underage worker at that time, Zhang found it extremely hard to get formal employment. At first he worked as a delivery boy for a washing-powder factory earning three hundred yuan per month. One year later, he managed to get formal employment in the same factory because his uncle worked there as a supervisor. With his uncle's help, Zhang's salary was increased to 360 yuan per month, which was higher than that of the other workers. Zhang told us that in the 1990s migrant workers were happy if they could earn two hundred to three hundred yuan per month. In addition to the low wages, job opportunities were scarce, as there was an excess supply of labor. Zhang recalled that in the 1990s, hundreds of migrant workers fought over jobs in labor-intensive factories, and many used personal connections to get such jobs. Job opportunities were so precious that workers rarely negotiated their pay and employment benefits with their employers.

In 1998, Zhang was working as a technician in the factory and earned eight hundred yuan per month, which was the best salary available on the shop floor. This was his golden year: he had a good job and was dating a girl from Sichuan province. He went to the girl's native village to meet her parents. The girl's parents opposed their union, because Zhang was not a Sichuan native. Many rural parents make it a condition that their children should marry a local spouse. After talking to his girlfriend's parents for a whole night, Zhang was unable to convince them and had to break up with her. Later, Zhang met his wife, a girl from a village near his own who also worked in Shenzhen, through the introduction of his relatives. The couple started dating shortly after being introduced and got married very quickly. In 2005, Zhang's wife gave birth to their first child, a daughter; six years later the couple had their second child, a son.

In 2013, Zhang was working as a security guard and earned twenty-five hundred to three thousand yuan per month, while his wife worked in an electronics factory. Zhang told us he did not like his job and considered it a dead end. He believed that factory work was more desirable than working as a security guard, because factory workers could learn skills, whereas security guards learned nothing from their work. As he stated, "If you work in a factory, regardless of what you do, you can learn some useful skills for your future development. If you have skills, then given a good opportunity, you may be promoted to technician or even team leader. But working as a security guard does not give you any skills. How can you learn something by just standing there and staring at the wall?" Zhang explained that he had to take this job because it was the only job that allowed him to visit his village frequently. Had he taken work in a factory he would not have had the leave he needed to visit his village every two to three months.

Zhang returned to his rural home so frequently because he had to help his father farm the land. His father had three siblings who had migrated to take work in cities. Zhang's father did not want the land to be left idle and wasted, so he insisted on farming the land belonging to all four families. Zhang was unwilling to be involved in farming and believed that the profit from it was small; nevertheless he still helped his father, because he worried that his father's health would be adversely affected by heavy farming. Zhang has an elder brother who married a wife from Hubei province and moved to Hubei to live with his in-laws. Zhang described his elder brother as "a married-out daughter," who could no longer be counted on to fulfill the son's responsibilities of looking after elderly parents and the family's land. Zhang believed that it was his responsibility to take care of his elderly parents and young children. In the face of his wife's objections to the frequent visits to his rural home, which adversely affected his earning power in the city, Zhang argued that his family was more important than money. As he told us, "Even if I did not make any money, I would still need to visit my family . I miss my children so much when I am in Shenzhen. My parents are old. . . . If I had not visited home to take care of them, I would feel very guilty . . . I told my wife, 'Do not use money to measure everything. That's meaningless.'" Zhang planned that he and his wife would stay in Shenzhen for another three to five years. When his parents got older, Zhang believed that either he or his wife would have to stay in the village to take care of his elderly parents and look after their children. Zhang had calculated the cost and profit from farming and optimistically estimated that he could earn fifty to sixty thousand yuan per year from farming. He believed that, given this income, he could support his family by farming even if he lost his job in Shenzhen. Zhang defined his life at the time we interviewed him as "falling short of the best, but better than the worst" (*bishang buzu bixia youyu*). In the interview he emphasized that money was not the most important thing in his life, and having a happy family and a peaceful life meant more to him.

RURAL-TO-URBAN MIGRATION AND CHINA'S MARKET TRANSITION IN THE 1980S AND 1990S

The stories of Feng and Zhang epitomize the experiences of China's internal migrant workers in the 1980s and 1990s. By 2013 the total number of migrant workers in China had reached 268.94 million (National Bureau of Statistics of PRC, 2014). The colossal waves of migration were the result of the Chinese government's engineering of economic development and the transition to a market economy that started in the late 1970s. After putting an end to the chaos of the Cultural Revolution, Deng Xiaoping, the paramount Chinese leader, and his allies realized that it was impossible to accomplish anything in a politically chaotic society, and that it was time to shift the state's focus from class struggle to economic development. Deng and his supporters believed that if they were to save people from poverty, rebuild the economic system paralyzed in the Cultural Revolution, and maintain the political legitimacy of the Communist Party, there was no alternative to transforming China's command economy and introducing market reforms. As Deng was to state frequently in the years that followed his first speech on the economic reform, "Poverty is not socialism" (*pinqiong bushi shehui zhuyi*), and "Development is the only hard truth" (*fazhan caishi ying daoli*). The Communist reformers of the post-Maoist era prioritized economic development and associated it with nation building and modernization. The deepening of the economic reforms, whose acknowledged goal was "Socialism with Chinese characteristics" (*youzhongguo tese de shehui zhuyi*), brought fundamental changes to many aspects of Chinese life; rural-to-urban migration is one of the most prominent.

In the prereform period the Chinese government left rural residents dependent on their own resources, because it had an urban-centered perspective on China's economic development and placed greater emphasis on the government's responsibility to provide permanent jobs, subsidized food and housing, and other social benefits for workers in state-owned enterprises and urban residents (Cheng and Selden, 1994). The *hukou* system was used to differentiate and segregate China's rural population from its urban counterpart and constrain the former's mobility and entitlement to social resources and benefits. Without an urban *hukou*, rural residents were not allowed to move to urban areas, look for jobs there, or even purchase food unless they got official permission in advance. The planned economy and the system for rationing food and important living resources guaranteed the effectiveness of the *hukou* system in constraining population movement (Cheng and Selden, 1994). Against this background, rural-to-urban migration in prereform China was limited and took place under strict constraints. In addition, both the government and urban citizens were aggressively hostile toward the migration of rural population. This hostility has not faded over the intervening decades, and it has had a significant impact on the lives and experiences of migrant workers in cities, despite the fact that mass rural-to-urban migration gradually became a constant of the postreform period.

China's economic reforms have transformed the economic system and social structures of the country and eroded the rigid rural-urban divide (Wong, 1994). The rural reforms of the late 1970s and 1980s decollectivized the land and increased food production, yet they also created a labor surplus in rural China (Li and Chui, 2011). In 1984, the central government issued the "Notice on Rural Work in 1984," which allowed rural people to move to urban areas for business or employment as long as they brought their own food and arranged their own accommodation (Wong, 1994; Wang, 2013). The Notice marked the start of the central government's official policy of loosening its tight control over rural population movement. In 1985 and 1986, the central government further loosened its control over rural to urban migration by canceling the unified state purchase and sale of major agricultural products and allowing state-owned enterprises to recruit rural labor (Wang, 2013). During this period the emergence of private businesses and a private economic sector created extra demand for labor. As a result a large number of rural residents poured into big cities, such as Shanghai, Guangzhou, and Nanjing, in what became the first wave of rural-to-urban migration. Estimates of the number of migrants in the second half of the 1980s range from thirty to seventy million, depending on the source.

A series of policies regulating and managing rural migrants' employment and residence in cities was established during this period. These policies allowed the government to maintain its control and surveillance of migrants. In 1985, for example, a nationwide system of temporary-residence permits (*zanzhuzheng*) was established by the Ministry of Public Security. This system required anyone aged sixteen or over who intended to stay somewhere outside his or her *hukou* registration area for more than three months to apply for a temporary-residence permit. The citizen identity card (*shenfenzheng*) system, which was implemented in tandem with the temporary-residence permit system, required all citizens aged sixteen or over to apply for an individual, portable identity card containing basic demographic information. These systems gave local governments the power to regulate rural-to-urban migrants, who were required to carry their temporary-residence permit, work permit, and citizen identity card and present them to the police on request. Migrant workers who could not present the required documents would face severe punishment, for example forced repatriation, implemented by local governments using the custody and repatriation system that was in place between 1982 and 2003.

In the 1980s both the central government and local governments in the receiving areas expected that rural-to-urban migrants would be sojourners or seasonal circulators, working in urban areas when needed and going back to their rural villages when their labor was considered redundant. This expectation was reflected in the labels initially given to rural-to-urban migrants in state discourse. Peasants who left their rural villages and migrated to urban areas for employment were not initially referred to as "migrants" or "migrant workers" (*nongmingong*). In the mid-1980s, when rural-to-urban migrants emerged as a new social group, they were officially referred to as the "floating population" (*liudong renkou*) or by the more negative term "blind drifters" (*mangliu*) (Wong, 1994). Seen as temporary and floating residents by the receiving areas, migrant workers were excluded from access to public services and welfare there. The majority migrated as individuals, leaving family members behind in their rural homes. They sought employment via fellow villagers (*laoxiang*), who constituted a vital support network. Migrants were housed either in crowded factory dormitories or in private housing provided by local residents, which was under the supervision of the police, to ensure that they remained under the control of urban governments.

Migrants' private lives were also under strict surveillance. In accordance with central government birth control policy, receiving cities such as Guangzhou and Shenzhen introduced birth control measures for married migrant workers as well as local residents. As Wong (1994) documented, after 1987 the Guangzhou government required married migrant workers to present a birth planning certificate issued by their home birth planning agency when they applied for a temporary residence permit. This policy was intended to prevent migrant workers from having "illegal" or "unscheduled" births in cities and thereby increasing the burden on urban governments. This web of government control and surveillance policies made it extremely hard, if not impossible, for migrants to bring their family to join them in the city, let alone start a new family and settle there.

Faced with increased numbers of rural-to-urban migrants, both central and local governments implemented stricter and harsher policies in the 1990s. The nightmarish Spring Festival of 1989, when hundreds of thousands of migrant workers crowded into the railway and bus stations of coastal cities, reflected the huge discrepancy between high migrant demand for public services and the serious undersupply of such services, including public transportation. The scenes during the Spring Festival not only caused the urban public to panic about the disorder that mass rural-to-urban migration might cause, it also led to tightening of government control over rural-to-urban migration. At the same time, far-reaching reform of state-owned enterprises led to an increase in the number of workers laid off and made unemployment a serious problem in many cities.

In the 1990s both central and local governments adopted a series of policies that restricted and monitored closely the so-called blind drifter populations in cities, although the central government claimed that the main aim of internal migration policy was "the orderly movement of rural labor under macroscopic regulation and control." In 1995, for example, the central government and the Ministry of Public Security introduced a unified system of work and temporary residence permits to regulate rural-to-urban migrants, and shortened the length of visits for which a temporary-residence certificate was required from three months to one month. To protect employment opportunities for people with urban *hukou*, many local governments in migrant-receiving cities implemented policies to restrict migrants' access to certain jobs (Li and Chui, 2011). For example, in the early 1990s the Guangdong government imposed very high penalties (three hundred yuan per person per day) on enterprises hiring nonlocal workers without its permission (Wong, 1994). Similarly, in 1998 the Beijing government produced a list of jobs that were not open to migrant workers and punished enterprises which violated this policy (Li, 2008). These regulations and policies forced migrant workers to the bottom of the urban labor market, which was dominated by so-called three-Ds jobs (dirty, dangerous, and difficult) that were shunned by urban residents.

Although rural-to-urban migration in the 1980s was mainly in the form of individual migration, family migration gradually increased, as migrant parents started to bring their children with them to cities in the late 1990s. At that time urban education resources were allocated in accordance with urban *hukou* registration, so urban governments did not take responsibility for the education of migrants' children. Without an urban *hukou*, migrants' children were not allowed to enroll in urban public schools. The dropout children of migrant workers became a prominent social problem, which the central government addressed with new policies. These dealt with the problem of educating migrant children on the one hand, and set up barriers to make it harder for them to migrate to cities on the other. In March 1998, the National Education Commission and the Ministry of Public Security jointly issued "Interim Regulations on the Education of Migrant Children." According to the Regulations only migrant children who had no guardian in their place of *hukou* registration were entitled to education where their migrant parents were living and working. At the same time, the Regulations required local governments in the sending areas to impose strict controls on the outward migration of school-age children. Public schools in receiving cities were also entitled to charge migrant children a relatively high tuition fee (*jiedufei*), whereas state education was almost free for children with an urban *hukou*. This tuition fee, which ranged from several thousand yuan to more than ten thousand yuan per year, was a formidable sum for most migrant parents, since they typically held low-income jobs; in effect it functioned to prevent migrant children from accessing education in cities. This may partly explain why many migrant parents chose to leave their children behind in rural China, thus causing another social problem, that of the so-called left-behind children (*liushou ertong*).

The impact of government policies on migrant workers and their families extends beyond the legal and administrative levels. As Castles and Miller (2003) pointed out, migration policies in receiving countries not only affect local people's attitudes toward migrants, they also shape the consciousness of migrants themselves. Although rural-to-urban migration in China is an internal migration, the institutional arrangements and structural inequalities that segregate rural and urban China have prompted scholars to dub it "one country, two societies" (Whyte, 2010). Myerson et al. (2010: 26) argued that differences "between rural and urban China are so pronounced that rural-to-urban migration is more like international labor migration between developing and developed countries than internal migration." Chinese urban governments' negative and restrictive policies on rural-to-urban migration in the 1980s and 1990s were the main factor in the low social status of migrant workers in urban areas; their low social status in turn shaped how they were treated by employers and perceived by urban residents. Many previous studies of migrant workers in China (e.g. Lee, 1998; Pun, 2005b) have demonstrated that in the 1980s and 1990s most migrant workers were employed in sweatshop factories characterized by long working hours, extremely low wages, oppressive working conditions, and inhumane management and disciplinary practices; they were also exploited by global capital and the socialist state.

During the 1980s and 1990s the mass media constructed a negative and discriminatory discourse directed against rural-to-urban migrants. They were either described as dirty, backward, uncivilized bumpkins who brought disorder, crime, and insanitary practices to urban areas, or depicted as docile, short-sighted, and ignorant but acquiescent maiden workers who needed the discipline of modern capitalism and urban culture (Pun, 2005a, b; Solinger, 1999). A popular TV series entitled *Rural Laboring Girls* (*wailaimei*) vividly documented the public image and life experiences of migrant workers in the 1980s and 1990s. At this time urban residents' attitudes to migrant workers were generally discriminatory and exclusive (Solinger, 1999). At worst, urban residents blamed migrant workers for the crowding on public transport, the increased crime rate, and the deterioration in public hygiene. At best, they kept a distance from migrant workers and segregated them both geographically and socially (Solinger, 1999). Given this social context, most migrant workers in the 1980s and 1990s treated migration to urban areas as a temporary stay rather than a permanent resettlement. For young, single girls from rural China, marriage usually meant the end of their migration and return to their rural home (Fan, 2008).

RURAL-TO-URBAN MIGRATION AND GOVERNMENT POLICIES IN THE NEW MILLENNIUM

As the new millennium began, internal migration in China entered a new stage. A prominent characteristic of migration in the new millennium has been the transformation in government policy, from constraining migration to guiding migration and protecting the rights and interests of migrant workers. The labor shortage that developed in the early 2000s may have been an important contributor to the policy transformation. Since 2003 the labor shortage has gradually swept across the Pearl River Delta and the Yangtze River Delta, the two main bases of labor-intensive factories, and it has now lasted for more than a decade. Between 2003 and 2014 it was estimated that Guangdong province, the primary destination for migrant workers, had a shortfall of two million workers (Choi and Peng, 2015). Although the labor shortage in other urban areas was not as serious as in the Pearl River Delta and the Yangtze River Delta, it nevertheless transformed the power relationship between capital and migrant labor in local labor markets (Peng and Choi, 2013; Choi and Peng, 2015).

Continual labor-shortage problems have not only attracted public attention, they have also become a key concern of the state. In the early 2000s the Chinese government redefined its development strategies to emphasize the importance of social stability and harmony (Li and Chui, 2011). Under the banner of "constructing a harmonious socialist society" (*jianshe hexie shehui*), the central government promoted its "people first" or "people-centered" (*yiren weiben*) approach and claimed to "solve problems concerning people's basic interests, enabling them to enjoy the fruits of reform and development more equally, as well as to gain from a strengthened democracy and legal system" (Li and Chui, 2011: 12). It was in this macropolitical context that a series of government policies to protect vulnerable social groups, including migrant workers, were developed and implemented.

Since the late 1990s the central government has gradually loosened its control over transfer of migrant workers' *hukou*. From the mid 2000s, migrant workers have been allowed to apply for *hukou* in medium and small cities if they have a stable job and residence there (Li and Chui, 2011). Another control system, the temporary-residence permit system, was scrapped in 2003 after Sun Zhigang, a graduate student from Hubei province who was looking for work in Guangzhou but was unable to provide a temporary-residence permit, was brutally beaten to death in a repatriation center where he was under detention. His death provoked public outrage against the custody and repatriation system (*shourong qiansong zhidu*) and the brutal enforcement methods used by the police; it also drew public attention to the suffering that inhumane government policies caused for millions of migrant workers. As a result of pressure from public opinion, the custody and repatriation system was scrapped and the temporary-residence permit system abolished. The abolition of these two systems had remarkable significance for migrant workers. It gave them the freedom to stay in urban areas even if they did not have formal employment, and they no longer had to be afraid of being detained and sent back to their rural home by government officials.

Over the following several years the central government gradually introduced various policies protecting the rights and interests of migrant workers, especially their labor rights. In 2003, the State Council released the "Notice on Doing a Better Job Concerning the Employment Management of and Services for Migrant Workers." This Notice stated that the employment and management of migrant workers should be governed by the principles of fair treatment, rational guidance, satisfactory management, and service improvement (Ngok, 2008). In 2004 the Ministry of Construction and the Ministry of Human Resources and Social Security jointly issued the "Circular on Managing Wage Payment to Migrant Workers in the Construction Sector," which was intended to address the problems with wage deduction and arrears that were prevalent in the construction industry (Pun and Lu, 2010a). In 2006 the State Council issued its first comprehensive policy document dealing with improvement of migrant workers' occupational and social status (Ngok, 2008). The main measures included ones that loosened the restrictions on migrant workers' application for a local household registration in medium and small cities, protected their labor rights and interests, provided compulsory education for their children in cities, and created infrastructure in rural areas.[1] These policies abolished various discriminatory regulations and unreasonable restrictions on migrant workers and emphasized that migrant workers should enjoy the same benefits and be treated in the same way as urban residents. In 2008 the central government's New Labor Contract Law came into effect; this made it mandatory for employers to sign written contracts with employees and was intended to standardize labor contracts and protect workers' rights and interests.

In response to central government advocacy of migrant workers' rights, local governments in the receiving cities have also introduced concrete policies that protect migrant workers' interests. Since 2005 the governments of major receiving cities in Guangdong province have

1. The policy document of the central government on migrant workers, 2006, http://www.china.com.cn/chinese/PI-c/1166619.htm

incrementally increased their minimum wages to force employers to raise migrant workers' salaries. In Shenzhen, Guangzhou, and Dongguan the minimum wage has been increased from 690 yuan, 684 yuan, and 574 yuan per month in 2005 to 1,808 yuan, 1,550 yuan, and 1,310 yuan per month in 2014, respectively. Local governments have also implemented other policies to safeguard migrant workers' welfare. For example in 2005 Shenzhen took the lead in implementing a medical insurance policy for migrant workers, and in 2009 the Guangdong government introduced a point system that enabled migrant workers to obtain local *hukou* in Guangdong province.

Since 2000 government policies on migrant workers' children have also been transformed. In September 2003 the State Council issued a policy document on providing compulsory education to the children of migrant workers. This document requires local governments and public schools in migrant-receiving cities to treat the children of migrant workers and urban citizens equally. In addition to forbidding urban public schools to charge so-called temporary schooling fees (*jiedufei*) for educating the children of migrant workers, the policy also required local governments to provide scholarships and fee exemptions for the children of migrant workers. In June 2006 an amendment to the Compulsory Education Law of the People's Republic of China enshrined in law that children of migrant workers had an equal right to compulsory education in urban areas. These protective government policies and regulations represented a break with the previous restrictive and discriminatory approach to migration. Most importantly, they made it easier for migrants to bring their families to cities. Rural-to-urban family migration has become more common in the new millennium.

There has also been gradual change in the demographic characteristics of the migrant worker population. In the late 1990s a new generation of migrant workers started to replace their parents; in the new millennium this group became the major labor force in the secondary labor market in the cities. The Chinese sociologist Wang Chunguang was the first to describe the phenomenon of the "new generation of migrant workers" (*xinshengdai nongmingong*), defining this cohort as migrants born after 1980 who started their first migration before they were twenty-five years old (Wang, 2001). Migrant workers of the new generation differ from their predecessors not only demographically—they are younger, better educated, and more likely to be single—but also in their motives for migration and their expectations of work and life in the cities (Pun and Lu, 2010b; Peng and Choi, 2013; Choi and Peng, 2015). The new generation was born after the rural economic reforms, so the majority grew up in rural families in relatively good material circumstances. After the 1980s the economic status of rural families improved markedly thanks to the rapid development of rural areas, increased government subsidies for rural families, and the abolition of the agricultural tax and other farm taxes. The hard work of their parents, the first generation of migrants, also contributed to the greater family well-being enjoyed by the new cohort of migrants during their upbringing. According to the China Rural Statistics Yearbook (2007), the average annual income for a rural Chinese family was 3,578 yuan per person in 2006, 2.2 times greater than the average annual income of a rural family in 1995, nine times greater than in 1986, and thirty-five times greater than in 1976.

As they grew up in wealthier families many young migrant workers never experienced economic hardship, nor did they have agricultural experience before migration. Not having heavy family economic burdens, these young migrant workers did not anticipate and were not ready to "eat bitterness" as their parents had done when working in the cities. In addition to economic gains, their motives for migration have also included personal development. Most of them expected that migration would give them more opportunities to acquire knowledge and skills, develop their career, or set up their own business as well as offering a better income than staying in their rural home. The new migrants were also eager to experience modern urban life. These goals meant that the new generation of migrant workers had higher expectations of salary and working and living conditions in cities than the first generation of migrant workers. A 2010 survey of the new generation of migrant workers in Shenzhen found that although they had, on average, expected a monthly income of forty-two hundred yuan, the actual average monthly income of respondents was only 1,838 yuan.[2] The huge discrepancy between what they had expected to be able to earn and what they were in fact able to earn partly explains the high employment turnover among young migrant workers; they changed job 0.63 times per year on average.[3] This high turnover in the labor market has contributed to the labor shortage in South China.

Young migrants' plans for their future have changed in line with the changes in motives for migration. Compared with the previous generation

2. The report on the new generation of migrant workers in Shenzhen, 2010, http://acftu.people.com.cn/GB/67582/12154737.html

3. Ibid.

of migrants, the members of the new generation tend to stay longer in the cities, and many of them are more determined to put down roots there (Pun and Lu, 2010b). While marriage usually meant the end of migration for the first generation of migrants, especially women, it is quite common for new generation of migrants to continue their journey after marriage. Many married couples either give birth to their children in the city or bring left-behind children to live with them there (Lan, 2014).

Despite the fact that in recent years the central government has gradually loosened its control over rural people's *hukou* transfer, and even promoted the settlement of migrant workers in medium and small cities, for most migrant workers it is still unrealistic to expect to settle in the city, especially in the case of big cities such as Shenzhen, Shanghai, and Guangzhou. Tight settlement criteria aside, housing prices in China's megacities have rocketed over the past decade and are beyond the reach of most migrant workers. Living costs in big cities are also soaring.

The new generation of migrant workers has faced a dilemma. Lacking agricultural experience and having become used to the colorful and rich urban life, most young migrant workers have found it hard to return to their rural home; they are not only bored by the monotonous rural life, but also reluctant to make a living by farming, as their parents or grandparents have done. They also find that the habits and lifestyle they acquired in the city, where there is more emphasis on individualism and consumption, are incompatible with many of the traditional values that still hold sway in rural China, where the emphasis is on collectivism and individual sacrifice for the welfare of the collective. Although better transportation and advanced communication technologies mean that cities and rural areas are now more connected, these new migrants have, paradoxically, found it harder to return to their rural home.

Nevertheless, no matter how many years they have lived in the city, and no matter how keen they are to become an urban resident, becoming fully integrated into a city has remained a distant goal for most migrants. The segregation of urban residents and migrant workers has always been cultural, economic, and social as well as legal and administrative. Without an urban *hukou*, migrants are still denied various social entitlements in cities, such as the right to purchase an apartment or apply for a car license. Despite the government policy shift on education for migrant children in the early 2000s, major migrant-receiving cities such as Guangzhou, Shenzhen, and Dongguan have not wholeheartedly implemented these policies. As a result, when we conducted our fieldwork between 2012 and 2015, many children of migrant workers in these cities were either enrolled in poor-quality private schools for migrant children, or their parents needed to pay a higher fee for them to be enrolled in public schools (Goodburn, 2009). Job markets in cities have remained segregated, with migrant workers being relegated to the lowest stratum. Their low income limits their options for rental housing and indirectly results in their need to crowd into villages in cities.

Young male migrant workers who do not have an urban apartment are undesirable mates in the urban marriage market. Even if they spend a large part of their income on fashionable clothes and advanced electronic devices so that they look and behave like urbanites, they remain a marginalized group in cities. Under these circumstances the new generation of migrants has struggled to decide whether to settle down in the city or return to the rural home they came from. This is particularly true for young male migrants, because of the traditional expectation that sons will take care of their parents in old age. The stories of Jiao and Ruan illustrate the experiences of many young male migrants in the new millennium. While single young male migrants are planning to find an ideal mate and develop their career, married young male migrants are more concerned about the well-being of their family.

JIAO: "MY DREAM IS HAVING A HAIR SALON IN DONGGUAN."

We met Jiao in Dongguan at the end of 2012. Born in 1992, Jiao is from Guangxi, a neighboring province of Guangdong. Jiao migrated for the first time when he was sixteen years old and found employment in a labor-intensive factory in Guangzhou. After working in Guangzhou for three years Jiao migrated to Dongguan in 2012, and found a job in a large ribbon factory. In a period of labor shortage it was quite easy for young migrant workers like Jiao to find employment in labor-intensive factories. Jiao changed jobs not because he wanted a higher salary, but in search of a brighter future. He wanted to visit more cities, gain more diverse work experience, and compare different cities to see which one would offer him the best opportunities for the future.

Jiao did not like his current job; he believed that nobody would like working in factories, as it meant losing autonomy and being constantly under managerial control. Jiao worked eight hours a day and had overtime work in peak seasons. He did not like overtime work and argued that workers should be able to rest after a regular eight-hour working day. Despite his dislike of factory work, Jiao stayed at the factory because he had made friends with a group of coworkers of the same age who shared his interests and hobbies. A more important reason for staying was that he was saving his salary for his dream, which was to become a hair stylist and open his own hair salon. Jiao was interested in personal image consultancy and had wanted to make it his career since high school. As he said, "In my high school, I noticed that many young people cared about their appearance very much. They discussed having a personal image designed to fit one's personality. I was young and one of them. I love personal image consultancy and would like to devote myself to this industry."

His experiences working in Guangzhou and Dongguan had led Jiao to believe that having one's own business was much better than working for others. Previously Jiao had apprenticed in a hair salon in Guangzhou as a step toward realizing his dream; however, being an apprentice was hard work, and apprentices were at the bottom of the salary and status hierarchy in the hair salon. Jiao admitted that he could not put up with being bullied by senior stylists and quit his job without becoming skilled in hair styling. This experience made him change his plan and decide to save the capital to open his own hair salon.

Jiao estimated that he needed to save at least fifty thousand yuan as start-up capital and planned to save two thousand yuan per month from his wage of around three thousand yuan per month as a factory worker. After working at the factory for around six months Jiao had saved only two thousand yuan in total, because he spent much of his income on socializing with his coworkers. Jiao realized that it would be hard to make his dream come true if he relied completely on his small income. His family was not able to provide much financial support. Jiao's parents endorsed his plan to open a hair salon and did not require him to send them remittances, but they were unable to provide any capital. Jiao finally found a coworker who was also interested in opening a hair salon, and they decided to collaborate to start their own business.

Jiao had dated two girls from work when he was in Guangzhou. In his late teens, dating was more like having fun than finding a marriage-able partner. Like many young men of that age, Jiao dated girls by chatting to them, taking them shopping and for meals. Jiao had sexual relationships with both girls, although he stated that the relationships had not been particularly affectionate. When asked whether they used protection when having sex, Jiao said: "We were very young at that time.

Young people love doing exciting things. Young people usually do not consider using that [a condom]." Jiao had told his first girlfriend about his dream of having a hair salon, but she was not supportive, because she believed that men working in hair salons were faithless and unreliable partners. Jiao did not believe he was faithless in love and was disappointed by her objections to his dream. They later broke up. When we met Jiao in Guangzhou, he was single and said he was not looking for a new girlfriend, because he was focusing on his career and needed to save money for his dream. Jiao told us that if he were able to have his own hair salon and become a successful man, finding a girlfriend would not be a problem.

Jiao defined ultimate success as being well fed and well clothed (*fengyi zushi*) and making people around him happy. Jiao had complicated feelings toward his rural home; he was attracted by and enjoyed the colorful urban life, but he missed the beautiful landscape of the village and his family. Yet despite declaring his love and emotional longing for his rural home, Jiao admitted that returning there is not part of his plans for the future.

RUAN: "I NEED TO WORK HARD FOR ANOTHER TEN YEARS."

Ruan was a twenty-seven-year-old restaurant owner when we met him in Guangzhou in March 2013. Ruan was from Hunan, another large migrant-sending province in China. Ruan migrated to Guangzhou when he was fifteen years old. He started as an apprentice in a Hunanese restaurant and worked there for two years to learn culinary skills. In his subsequent years in Guangzhou Ruan has shifted between running his own restaurant and working as a cook in other people's restaurants.

In 2005 Ruan invested all his savings, between forty and fifty thousand yuan, in his first Hunanese restaurant, but he closed it down two years later because of high rents. After that he worked as a cook for three years until he made his second attempt to set up his own restaurant, in 2007. The restaurant was around one hundred square meters, with a rent of eighty-five hundred yuan per month, and could seat ten tables with around forty customers. To keep costs down Ruan had hired only eight employees. Ruan and his wife worked longer and harder than their staff. Ruan worked from seven o'clock in the morning to eleven o'clock at night, fulfilling several roles. He was merchandiser, cook, waiter, cashier, and cleaner, as necessary. Although running a restaurant was exhausting, Ruan still planned to open another one if his current one was a success and made good money.

Ruan met his wife in 2003, when both of them were working at the same restaurant. His wife is also from Hunan. Ruan recalled the simple happiness they once had: "I have a very fond memory of the time we spent together [during their courtship]. At that time, neither she nor I made much money. But, we were very happy. Society then was simple, not materialistic. There was no social pressure [on men] to buy a car or an apartment. I could make her happy and satisfied by just buying her a bottle of Coke."

Ruan and his wife got married in 2007 and had a five-year-old daughter when we met him. Ruan's family responsibilities placed great pressure on him, especially when he compared his life with the lives of his friends in his rural home. As he said, "If I stop thinking about the material stuff, such as the house and the car, I can be very happy. But, when I notice my friends all have houses and cars, I feel contempt for myself. I ask myself, 'why can't you measure up to that level?' I put the pressure on myself. Last year, I went back to my home village during the Spring Festival and observed that my friends all had their own businesses there. Some were running a restaurant; some had opened a hair salon, and some sold clothes. And they all had houses there. They seemed to have a good life. I asked myself, 'What do you have after working in Guangzhou for over ten years?' And I decided to work harder for another ten years to make a better life." Ruan invested all his savings in his business, so he has not built a house in his village, which is not considered acceptable in a married son in rural China. Ruan's account illustrates clearly how the pressure migrant men feel is derived from comparing their struggles in the city with the life of men staying behind.

Ruan considered it natural that he and his wife shared housework and the care of their five-year-old daughter, because both of them worked long hours in the restaurant. In the morning, Ruan would take his daughter to kindergarten before returning to the restaurant or going to the market. In the afternoon he went to pick her up. Ruan's wife would take her home while Ruan stayed behind until the restaurant closed. For Ruan, sharing housework and child-care responsibilities was pragmatic rather than problematic, given the demands of the restaurant; nonetheless he aspired to a future in which he could support his wife to be a full-time, middle-class urban housewife who could enjoy her leisure time. He promised her that after he opened a few more restaurants, she would have a comfortable life and would be able to enjoy leisure activities such as going shopping, having coffee, and playing cards with her friends.

Ruan's aspirations for his wife reflected his own image of the life of a rich man's wife in urban China rather than his wife's wishes. Ruan's wife had told him that she would be happy as long as the business was doing well and they were making money. She had also told him that she did not need him to be rich; she cared more that he should be in good health and stay loyal to their marriage. Having lived in cities for more than ten years, Ruan's understanding of successful manhood was shaped by urban discourses that define masculinity primarily in terms of men's entrepreneurial success and ability to provide a comfortable, middle-class life for their family. Although the family's economic circumstances made it essential that Ruan's wife worked as hard as he in their small business and that they shared duties at work and at home, whenever he could Ruan tried to "perform masculinity" by letting his wife spend more time with their daughter. During weekends, for example, Ruan would try to avoid asking his wife to work at the restaurant, so that she could take their daughter to playgrounds, or to have Japanese or Korean food in shopping malls, or to see a movie. Ruan believed that to be considered a successful man by his friends and to provide a comfortable life for his family, he would need to work hard for another ten years. He repeated this several times in the interview. Until he can achieve real success, he has to compromise his ideal gender norm of "men outside, women inside" (the Chinese equivalent of the male provider/female homemaker in Western societies) by having his wife work alongside him in their small business. The two of them have to work hard both inside and outside their home.

CONCLUSION

Feng, Zhang, Jiao, and Ruan are marginal yet ordinary male rural-to-urban migrants in postreform China. Their stories and their families' changing circumstances reflect the grand economic and social transformation China has experienced over the past three-and-a-half decades. Today China is a formidable force on the world's economic and political stages. In China's megacities, such as Shenzhen and Guangzhou, and in buzzing economic zones such as the Pearl River Delta, glittering high-rises and shopping malls full of Western luxury products rub shoulders with the many "villages in cities" that have sprung up to house the millions of rural-to-urban migrant workers and their families.

Underpinning the nation's grand narrative of development and modernization are the sweat, hard work, endless sacrifice, and aspirations of these migrants and their families. The stories of individual migrants and of the first cohort of migrant workers have been told; however much less is known about how China's great transformation has affected the new generation of rural-to-urban migrants and their families. Even less is known about how migrant couples and migrant families cope with and manage the impact of migration on family life. This chapter has used the narratives of four ordinary migrant men, belonging to two distinct phases of China's reform era, to relate the impact of rural-to-urban migration on family and gender in postsocialist China to the broader structural transformations the country has undergone. The interweaving of personal stories and grand narratives reminds us that although there is a theoretical distinction between personal and structural changes, on the ground it would be difficult to disentangle them.

In a society where family has traditionally played a central role in shaping the lives and well-being of individual family members, rural-to-urban migration is seldom an individual decision. It is often a family strategy based on income maximization and risk diversification. This means that both the migrants and their stay-behind family are affected by migration; their lives, in urban and rural China respectively, are reshaped. Gender and intergenerational relationships within the families of millions of rural-to-urban migrants are negotiated. Migrant men have to resolve the tension between urban discourses of successful manhood, which emphasize men's financial power, and the reality of their precarious economic existence at the margins of urban society. They also need to negotiate their multiple family roles and gender identity to meet the changing standards for attractive lovers, good husbands, responsible fathers, and filial sons. In the following chapters we discuss how the migration of rural men has reframed their romantic relationships, conjugal dynamics, paternal duties, and filial obligations. While China is marching toward modernity, these rural-to-urban migrant men are journeying through life as lovers, husbands, fathers of left-behind children, and sons of stay-behind elderly parents. And here and there the path of the nation and the journeys of these marginal men intersect.

CHAPTER 3

Striking a Balance

Courtship, Sexuality, and Marriage

Bian was working as a bartender in a hotel in Guangzhou when we interviewed him in March 2013. He is from Meizhou, a city in northeastern Guangdong, which is regarded as less developed than the Pearl River Delta. Born in 1982, Bian is the only son and the elder brother of two sisters in his family. After finishing junior high school, Bian dropped out of school, as he had lost interest in studying and thought that it would be a waste of his father's money to continue. After dropping out of school, Bian migrated to Guangzhou. After changing jobs several times in the first two years, Bian worked as a delivery man for his cousin's business; he met his first girlfriend, a cashier, there.

Bian's first girlfriend was a pretty girl from Guangxi province who was one year older than him. Bian told us that he did not initiate the relationship. It was his girlfriend who had made the first move. Bian claimed that as a good-looking man, he had always been popular with girls and did not need to learn how to pursue them. Bian's first girlfriend was his ideal type of woman: she was mature, caring, and good at socializing. Bian confessed that he liked mature women (*shunv*) and found his first girlfriend charming, as she was pretty good at taking care of others and socializing. Being one year older than Bian, this girl took good care of him by cooking, doing laundry for him, and helping him in his work. Bian enjoyed her attention and enjoyed being cared for. After they had been living together for a while Bian had decided to marry her. He mailed the girl's picture to his parents and also provided them with her name, place of origin, and lunar date of birth.

But before they had even met their future daughter-in-law in person and had a chance to get to know her, Bian's parents had already disapproved of his marriage plan, because according to the traditional Chinese horoscope, Bian and his girlfriend had incompatible *bazi*. Calculating the *bazi* (an eight-character representation of one's date of birth in terms of year, month, date, and hour in the traditional Chinese calendar) of bride and groom is an important procedure in traditional Chinese marriage. According to ancient Chinese astrology, one's *bazi*, the information carried by one's birth date, can determine one's personality, talent, and even fate. According to traditional Chinese marriage lore, if a woman's *bazi* is incompatible with that of her fiancé they are not destined to be a couple. Should they marry, not only will the couple be unhappy, but their marriage will bring bad luck to the husband's family. Although the influence of traditional marriage lore has faded in many urban areas of China since 1949, it still carries a lot of weight in rural China. In addition to their incompatible *bazi*, the practical and more important reason that Bian's parents objected to his marriage plan was that his girlfriend was from Guangxi, which was a remote place in the eyes of his parents, who wanted a local daughter-in-law. Although Bian was not convinced by his parents' reasoning, he accepted their opinion and broke up with his girlfriend. She went back to her rural home in Guangxi, married another man, and Bian gradually lost contact with her. Recalling his first romantic relationship more than a decade later, Bian regretted that he did not fight for their relationship or cherish the girl who had once looked after him so well.

After breaking up with his first girlfriend, Bian dated several other girls from different provinces and cohabited with two of them; however, he did not treat these relationships as seriously as his relationship with his first girlfriend. This is perhaps because Bian had realized after his first failed relationship that his parents would never allow him to marry a nonlocal girl that he met during migration. Gradually, Bian seems to have accepted his parents' view that marrying a nonlocal girl would be problematic. As he told us,

> Marrying a local girl is more convenient as all the relatives live nearby . . . whereas marrying a nonlocal woman is troublesome. If I had married a nonlocal woman, I would have to accompany her to visit her parents in another province, which would cost me a lot financially. I would need to pay for transport, and buy gifts for her parents and relatives during every visit. I

might also need to give her parents money for every Chinese festival. On the contrary, marrying a local girl makes life simpler. In our village, giving parents-in-law one thousand yuan at every spring festival is enough.

In 2011 Bian married a local girl chosen by his parents. One year later, his wife gave birth to a son. Although this marriage satisfied his parents' wish for a local daughter-in-law, Bian did not find much passion in his marriage, since his wife does not fit his ideal type of woman. Rather than being nurturing and taking good care of her husband, Bian's wife seems to prefer a more egalitarian conjugal relationship. She always asks Bian to share the housework, including the laundry and cooking. Bian admitted that he was a traditional man, who believed that all housework was women's work, and refused to share it with her. Their disagreement about the division of household labor was an ongoing cause of conflict.

Bian's struggle to reconcile his city experiences of romantic love with the pressure to meet rural Chinese parental expectations for a marriage partner was typical of our younger male respondents. For younger men, leaving their rural home and embarking on the adventure of city living has not only meant finding employment in factories or the service sector, it has also meant becoming familiar with urban life and its increasingly Westernized values of love, romance, sex, choice, and desires (Ma and Cheng, 2005). Although romance and love are regarded as vital components of an intimate relationship or marriage in Western societies, they are seen as subordinate to the needs of family in traditional Chinese societies (Moore and Leung, 2001). Prior to the enactment of the 1950 Marriage Law by the Chinese Communist Party, most Chinese marriages were arranged in accordance with the wishes of the parents (Xu and Whyte, 1990). Marriage in traditional Chinese societies was regarded primarily as a means of "connecting the political, social, and economic resources between the two families, rather than a result of love and affection between the two married parties" (Sheng, 2005: 102). Consequently, the existence of a romantic bond between the couple was regarded as unimportant; moreover, dating was uncommon, because contacts between single men and women were not allowed, and single young women were supposedly to be secluded in the inner quarters of the home (Mann, 2011). Shortly after coming to power in 1949 the Chinese Communist Party enacted the Marriage Law. The 1950 Marriage Law sought to break the traditional patriarchal shackles on women and increase the autonomy of married couples, by emphasizing that young people had the freedom to choose their own marriage partners and promoting love-based marriage as the ideal (Davis, 2014). The Marriage Law asserted that marriage should be between willing partners, based on love, and should not be subject to control or intervention by any third party. Notwithstanding the fact that the Marriage Law had given legal backing to companionate marriage based on romantic love, dating opportunities for young people in the socialist period were limited (Farrer, 2002). This does not mean, however, that under socialism Chinese youth were incapable of experimenting with sex and intimacy. According to Honig (2003) love affairs, secret romances, and premarital sex were common among sent-down youth[1] during the Cultural Revolution, in spite of being prohibited by the state and its local agents. The 1980s economic reforms gave Chinese youth further scope to pursue romance, love, and sex. These changes have been documented in rich ethnographic studies of both rural and urban China. Jankowiak (1993) described Chinese expectations about emotions, marriages, and sex in the 1980s on the basis of fieldwork carried out in Huhhot, the capital of Inner Mongolia. Jankowiak reported that courtship, informal dating, flirting, romantic involvement, and sexual seduction were prevalent among young people and documented significant sex differences in romantic fantasies and mating preferences. Chinese men's romantic fantasies focused on an idealization of female physical beauty, whereas Chinese women's romantic fantasies were more concerned with "the potential interactional qualities of the involvement" (Jankowiak, 1993: 220). When it came to mating preferences, Chinese men tended to regard their female mates as sexual objects, whereas Chinese women viewed men as status objects. Similarly, in an ethnographic study of family changes in a northeastern rural village in the second half of the last century, Yan (2003: 9) reported that under the influence of the market economy and urban consumption culture, "the notions of romantic love, free choice in spouse selection, conjugal independence, and individual property" had gradually become "important in the domestic sphere" in rural China and that normative discourses relating to romance and ideal spouses had altered accordingly. The characteristics of the ideal husband in the socialist period—a decent and reliable man (*laoshi*)—lost their appeal. Where previously

---

1. "Sent-down youth" were young people who, either voluntarily or coerced, left urban centers to live and work in rural areas as part of the Communist Party's "Up to the Mountains and Down to the Countryside Movement," from the beginning of the 1950s to the end of the Cultural Revolution.

men had been valued for their physical strength and farming ability, in postreform rural China the ability to earn good money in a nonagricultural job, good looks, eloquence, and emotional expressiveness became the new standards by which potential husbands were judged. In contrast, the dominant view of what constituted an ideal wife did not seem to change much. Having a good personality, for example, and being filial and hardworking, have remained at the core of a peasant man's concept of a virtuous wife. Another prominent change in rural young people's experience of romance and marriage was "the increased intimacy in and post engagement actions" (Yan, 2003: 84), such as romantic talk and premarital sex.

In a study of changes in the sexual culture of urban China between the 1980s and 2000 in Shanghai, a cosmopolitan city on the country's east coast, Farrer (2002) argued that the opening up of China and its adoption of a market economy had shifted people's focus from national construction and class struggle to market logic and principles. As state monitoring of personal lives became less obtrusive, a new social context developed in urban China, a context in which young people could explore new ideas about romance and sexuality. The emergence of dating and premarital sex, and the loosening of the connection between courtship and marriage, reflected an emphasis, among urban youth in postreform China, on the feelings, pleasures, and autonomy of the individual in romantic and sexual relationships.

While some scholars have highlighted the transformations in the dating practices, sexual behavior, and marriage patterns of young people in postreform China, other scholars (e.g. Ma and Cheng, 2005; Friedman, 2000) have emphasized the resilience of traditions and their continuing constraining influence on young people's romantic and sexual behavior. In a study of Huian women's romantic and sexual behavior in rural Fujian in the mid-1990s, Friedman (2000) argued that in spite of the growing popularity of romantic love among rural youth and the gradual emergence of premarital sex and cohabitation, rural women who had premarital sex, cohabited, or talked about sexual pleasure were still criticized by the older generation. The dominant local discourse on marriage and sexual intimacy remained very traditional; they were still strongly associated with reproduction rather than being considered in the context of young people's emotional needs and sexual desires. Similarly, Yan (2003) noted that in the rural northeastern village where fieldwork for the study was carried out, premarital sex was only regarded as acceptable for engaged couples. It was the engagement ritual and the couple's commitment to a foreseeable marriage that legitimated sexual intimacy. Ma and Cheng (2005:322) argued that although the mass internal migration that has taken place since the 1980s had given young people from rural areas more opportunity to pursue romantic love, "tradition employs gossip, discrimination, myth and moral values to discipline [them]." For many young migrant women, falling in love with a man outside the local community is romantic, but finding a husband close to home through matchmaking is still "a pragmatic strategy of self-protection" (Ma and Cheng, 2005: 322). Thus, rather than completely rejecting Chinese marriage traditions, young migrants struggle to reconcile their pursuit of modernity with observance of tradition.

Most extant Chinese ethnographic research on gender and sexuality focuses on women's suffering and experiences, and ignores men's voices, perspectives, and subjective experiences of intimate heterosexual relationships. Jankowaik (2006) argued that defining men and women respectively as the dominant and subordinate partners in intimate heterosexual relationships meant that romantic relationships were always viewed through the lens of gender, while the influence of social class and economic status remained underexplored. In this chapter we analyze the transformation in young migrant men's experiences of intimacy, romance, and sex, and explore their liminal status. We focus on the following specific research questions: how does rural-to-urban migration shape rural young men's ideology and practices with regard to romance and sex? How does urban consumerism affect their dating practices and sexual relationships? How do they handle the conflict between their romantic idealism and their obligations to obey parental wishes related to their marriage?

MIGRATION: A NEW ROAD TO ROMANCE

If, as Yan (2003) argued, market reforms have gradually changed the discourses on romance, intimacy, and the ideal spouse in rural China, it is equally true that the migration of rural youth to urban areas has accelerated these transformations and thrust these young migrants into urban modernity in a direct and dramatic way. Gaetano (2008: 630) argued that rural-to-urban migration has given rural youth the "space and conditions for exercising greater autonomy in choosing marital partners and conducting courtship." Working in the city and staying away from parental surveillance gives young migrants the time and space to experience modern life, and the financial independence they gain gives them more opportunity to experience the romance and intimacy of which they have dreamed. Falling in love and dating have become an indispensable part of their migration experience and a part of the process of growing up and discovering oneself and one's sexuality (Moore and Leung, 2001). Because millions of young migrants are employed in labor-intensive factories, construction sites, and service industries, and live mainly in industrial zones and "villages in cities," they have ample opportunity to interact and socialize with migrants of the opposite sex who are the same age and have similar backgrounds and life experiences. Being part of a large group of migrant peers working and living together increases the chances of finding suitable mates and creates the perfect environment in which to become involved in a romantic relationship. Spatial and social proximity in workplaces have been identified as significant factors in the development of relationships (Farrer, 2014), so it was unsurprising that many of our respondents had dated coworkers. For example, Xiao Ge, a twenty-seven-year-old man working in a shoe factory in Guangzhou, had dated four girls from work. When asked why he had chosen to date those girls, Xiao Ge said matter-of-factly, "We were always together. We always had fun together and we got along well. So, we dated." A twenty-year-old young man, Jiao, who worked in a ribbon factory, also found his first girlfriend at work. He explained, "We worked on the same shop floor of the same factory. We worked together every day, and we dated."

We should also remember that certain aspects of romance and sexuality have been commercialized in cities (Jacka, Kipnis, and Sargeson, 2013). The colorful urban nightlife experiences in the dancing squares, discos, pubs, cafes, and skating rinks provide young migrant men with opportunities to meet girls. Gui, a twenty-eight-year-old plumber working in Dongguan, met his first girlfriend at a skating rink in 2004, when he was nineteen years old. As he recalled,

> When I met my first girlfriend in a skating rink . . . I was unsophisticated. At that time, she did not have a phone, but I had one. I gave her my mobile number. The next day, she called me. And then we met regularly. I took her out to the pubs, to my friends' gatherings and to see the sea. We dated for a year.

As Gui mentioned, young migrants' widespread adoption of modern communication technologies such as mobile phones has made it easier for young migrant men to stay in contact with girls. It has also created new ways to meet potential romantic partners. Some reported that they had met girlfriends online. Yim, a twenty-five-year-old man working in a shoe factory in Guangzhou, told us he had met his second girlfriend via QQ, a popular instant-messaging service for young people in mainland China:

> We chatted online. I got her cell phone number through our QQ chat. One day, I was hanging out. Coincidentally, she was hanging out at the same place. I gave her a call and knew that she was in the same place as me. So, we met. And gradually, we got to know each other better and dated.

For most young migrant men, dating girls is a learning process, a way of learning how to get along with the opposite sex and establish a romantic relationship. It is also one of the ways in which they learn how to be a man. Young migrant men split girls into two categories—those who are ideal girlfriends or lovers, and those who are virtuous wife material. They are similar to their older counterparts in placing moral criteria, such as filial piety and hard work, at the heart of their concept of virtuous wifehood; however, they also stressed that they valued mutual passion and spiritual communication with their girlfriends and lovers. Three migrant men aged thirty, twenty-six, and nineteen years old, respectively, expressed this in different ways:

> My ideal mate is the girl I broke up with last year. She is ten years younger than me . . . but we have that kind of soul consonance with each other. When I looked at her eyes and she looked at my eyes, we could read each other's minds. She would know what I wanted or what I wanted to say through one simple gesture of mine. We are soul mates. Of all the girls I have seen and dated, she is the only one who could read my mind. And I could also read hers.

> I fell in love with that girl at first sight. It was a feeling I don't know how to express. When I was working in the kitchen, she, dressed in a black suit, came in and led a group of people to check up on work. When I first saw her, my heart beat very fast and I had no eyes for anyone else.

> My ideal girlfriend would be compatible with me in personality. . . . I don't like those introverted girls. I like extroverted, cheerful girls.

Although most of our respondents considered physical attractiveness secondary to moral character in a good wife, they talked about how they were attracted to pretty girls they dated. Their standards of female beauty were very orthodox, placing emphasis on a tall and slender frame, long hair, and delicate facial features. Migrant men's dissociation between the categories of "girlfriend" and "wife" reflects their acceptance, even internalization, of the modern, urban ideology of romantic love, which was defined by Giddens as a "pure relationship," in which partnership and commitment are established through individual choice rather than institutional bondage, and which is based primarily on compatibility of personalities and physical attraction (Giddens, 1991). Growing up after the market reforms took effect, these young migrant men might have been exposed, through popular culture and mass media, to the Western discourse of romantic love before they migrated to the city. As Ng, a twenty-eight-year-old migrant worker, recalled, "[Before migration,] we always dreamed about how beautiful and fantastic urban life would be. We dreamed of the neon glamour and crazy nightlife in cities. Our perceptions of urban life were heavily influenced by Hong Kong TV dramas of the 1980s." When they migrated, these young men were impatient for their first experience of urban romance. Jiao, a twenty-year-old migrant man, told us that "finding a girlfriend is something you must do. We are young boys. We have fun dating girls." This resonates with Farrer's (2002) research on what dating meant to the urban youth of Shanghai. According to Farrer (2002: 160), "While dating retained the purpose of finding a mate, it was also matter of proving one's desirability, having fun, and enjoying the attention of the opposite sex before marriage."

Compared with their predecessors, who often migrated after getting married in rural China, the younger male migrants we interviewed have had a more active romantic life and richer dating experiences. Twenty-five of the 107 migrant men under thirty-five years old that we interviewed reported that they had dated two or three girls since migrating. Fourteen reported having had four or more romantic relationships. Their relatively rich dating experience showed that these young men, their rural backgrounds and marginalized economic position notwithstanding, were eager to demonstrate their masculine charm in an urban context. Some bragged in interviews about the difficulties of juggling too many admirers, and the problems they had getting rid of enthusiastic female pursuers. They were not embarrassed to define themselves as "bad boys" or "playboys." Wan, a thirty-two-year-old hair stylist, bragged to the interviewer,

> It is very troublesome when so many girls are interested in me. I used to blind date with five girls on the same day. On my birthday, three girls who were interested in me came to my place to celebrate my birthday. I had to make plans to keep them away from each other and I met them in three different places.

Regardless of whether Wan's claim is true or false, his words attest to his view that being popular with women was a desirable attribute that he could share proudly with the interviewer. Popularity with women in urban China is, nevertheless, costly, because dating and consumption have become an inescapable part of the urban lifestyle. This is particularly challenging for migrant men, because dating is a gendered process. Men are expected to pay most of the girl's expenses on a date. This is one of the ways in which men assert their masculinity: by proving their financial superiority over a female partner, and demonstrating their willingness to be her protector and supporter. Yet most migrant men earn a meager salary and can barely keep up with the soaring living costs in urban China, never mind compete with the spending power of their much more affluent urban counterparts.

DATING, CONSUMPTION, AND BREAKUP

As Farrer (2002) indicated, the sexual culture and romantic discourse in postreform China arose in a macroinstitutional context, in which the capitalist labor market and the consumer market are the biggest influences, playing a significant role in shaping people's ideologies and practices with respect to love, intimacy, and sexual behavior. Urban China's fast-expanding market economy and consumer market meant that dating and romance quickly became associated with consumption. Commercialization of leisure and entertainment gave people new stages on which to express their emotional and sexual desires (Farrer, 2002). The mass media and the commercial world have acted in concert to teach young men that romance involves buying expensive gifts for their girlfriends, treating them to nice meals, taking them to theaters, discos, bars, and cafes, and planning activities to celebrate the various Chinese and Western festivals. Men's financial role in dating is not just a way of winning the hearts of desirable women, but a way of displaying their masculinity and gaining face. In other words, in urban romantic culture a man's romantic credentials depend to a large extent on how much money he is willing and able to spend on his girlfriend. When asked which party should be responsible for the bill on a date, 58 percent of our 192 male informants believed that it was the man's responsibility to pay the bill on a date with a girl. About 11 percent of them could not decide on this matter, and 30.7 percent thought the bill should be split equally or that the girl should sometimes reciprocate and treat the man. In discussing their romantic experiences, many men related them to consumption and entertainment activities. Mak, a security guard in his early thirties, told us, "When my friend and I wanted to date two girls, we took them out to have fun. We took them to fairgrounds, skating rinks, and karaoke bars. Sometimes, we took them to a barbecue."

Another interviewee, Tang, a thirty-one-year-old shop-floor worker, recalled that his most romantic experience had been presenting his girlfriend with a gold necklace as a birthday gift:

> The happiest time in our relationship was when we were passionately in love with each other. The happiest and most impressive memory is on her birthday that year, I bought her a gold necklace. She was so moved that she burst into tears when I presented it to her.

Conducting a romance through the medium of consumption is inescapably dependent on economic power. In cities migrant workers have always been the lowest income group due to the rural-urban divide, *hukou* discrimination, and the generally low wage levels in the secondary labor market in which they are marooned. Around 72 percent of the 192 migrant men we interviewed received a monthly salary of less than 3,999 yuan. Set alongside the living expenses of cities like Dongguan, Guangzhou, and Shenzhen, which averaged 2,771 yuan, 2,763 yuan, and 2,401 yuan per month respectively,[2] the income of these migrant men was barely sufficient to cover their own basic spending, let alone support regular, expensive, romance-related consumption. For example, Mak told us that he visited bars and restaurants on a weekly basis, and as a direct result had no savings at all at the end of every month. He referred to himself as one of the "moonlight clan" (*yueguangzu*). For most male migrants a taste of the urban romantic experience, complete with "fancy" consumption and entertainment, is possible once in a while, but unrealistic on a regular basis. They may behave generously and consume ostentatiously in front of girls in order to attract their attention and demonstrate masculine charm; however, when they start dating a girl regularly and hang out with her frequently, urban consumption habits become a burden and may even cause them embarrassment in front of their girlfriend. Yim's experience vividly illustrates the awkward situation in which most young migrant men find themselves. In 2013 Yim was working as a shop-floor worker in a shoe factory, earning a monthly salary of between four and five thousand yuan. In 2012 he had dated a Hunanese girl who worked as a salesperson. Yim felt under great pressure while they were dating, because of the discrepancy between his salary and his girlfriend's consumption habits. Yim observed that the stuff his girlfriend bought and used was much more expensive than his. He guessed that his girlfriend might be from a

2. http://www.mallchina.org/BusEnvironment/EnvironmetDetail/1100

well-off family or have a higher income than he. When Yim and his girlfriend went out together he felt uncomfortable, even when she was very thoughtful and did not ask him to purchase expensive gifts for her or take her to fancy restaurants. As a result he lacked confidence in their relationship:

> When we went shopping together, she deliberately picked something inexpensive. She knew my financial situation. When she shopped with me, she did not buy the stuff she usually purchased. She bought the cheap stuff which she would not buy when shopping alone. Frankly speaking, I was touched by her consideration.

Shanghai girls in Farrer's (2002) study used the amount of money a man was willing to spend on them as a measure of how seriously he treated the relationship. In an urban dating culture that mixes romantic idealism with pragmatic materialism (Farrer, 2014; Zhang and Sun, 2014), demonstrating generosity through high spending in dating contexts has become the new barometer of manhood. Yim considered changing his job, so that he would be better able to meet his girlfriend's standards of consumption and thus measure up to the urban ideal of a good boyfriend. He assumed that being a salesman would bring him more income, and sound more respectable than a shop-floor worker, but before he was able to find a better job his girlfriend broke up with him. She told Yim that her parents objected to their dating, so she had to break up with him. Yim was sad when he heard this, but what made him sadder still is that he did not know how to respond to her words. As he told us,

> When my ex-girlfriend broke up with me using this reason, I really did not know how to face it and respond. If I want to keep her and persuade her parents, what should I say? What could I promise or offer? What if they ask: "Do you have a house? What savings do you have?" I did not know how to answer those questions because I could not promise anything for their daughter.

In postsocialist China, hypergamy remains the explicit marriage norm for women in both rural and urban areas, since men are expected to be better off than, or at least of equivalent status to, their wives in terms of education, occupation, and income (Yan, 2003; Zhang and Sun, 2014). Men and their parents are still expected to provide a house for the young married couple. The questions Yim imagined his ex-girlfriend's parents asking were quite normal. Yim's awareness that he lacked the financial capital and breadwinning capacity to be able to give satisfactory answers to these questions weakened his confidence when it came to dating and marriage. After he broke up with his girlfriend Yim's friends introduced him to two other girls. However, Yim was not much interested in dating them. As he said, "When I realized that I was not economically capable of dating those girls, I was in no mood to devote myself to those relationships."

While Yim's frustration was rooted in his economic incapability to entertain and support his girlfriend's consumption habits, some migrant men's disheartenment derived from their economic inferiority to other men. Dating girls involves competing with other men for desirable partners. In modern capitalist societies a man's economic power is generally his most powerful weapon against his romantic rivals. Ng, a twenty-eight-year-old migrant working as a deputy director in a labor-intensive factory, told us the story of a young migrant man whose romantic dream was destroyed by another man's wealth. Ng is from Henan Province in central China, and he migrated to Dongguan in 2004 after he graduated from high school. In 2005 he was working as a shop-floor worker in a factory and had his first serious relationship, with a girl from Hunan. As he recalled,

> I liked her at first sight because her hairstyle impressed me. She tied her hair like Wang Fei [a pop singer]. Do you remember how Wang Fei tied her hair when she sang the song *Dating in 1998* at the Spring Festival Gala?. . . At that time, she was pursued by several other men. I defeated those rivals by devoting all my time and my heart to her. We worked together on the shop floor. I accompanied her to lunch. I spent all my leisure time with her after we got off work. I devoted myself to her.

In 2008, after they had been together for three years, Ng made plans to marry his girlfriend. He did not anticipate that at this point he would be defeated by another man's money. When he proposed, his girlfriend said to him, "If you can drive a BMW, why would you want to ride a bike?" It turned out that when his girlfriend returned home in 2008, her father had lined up a wealthy local owner of a coal mine as her prospective husband. Ng attempted to save their relationship by going to the girl's home village to meet her family. Predictably, he received a frosty reception, and his former girlfriend said to his face, "I will not marry you." Ng was so devastated that he immediately returned to his rural home and asked his parents to arrange a marriage for him. In 2009 he married a local girl he does not like at all, who was introduced by one of his aunts. Ng admitted that his ex-girlfriend had hurt him so deeply with her insulting words that he had lost faith in romance and marriage. As he said,

Her words devastated me. I suddenly realized that people were so materialistic and instrumental in this world. After I broke up with her, I felt drowsy all the day and lost my interest in everything. I was very passive. My understanding of romance and marriage was altered. I thought marriage was just finding a woman and having a baby with her. It did not matter whom I married as long as my parents were happy. Since my parents did not want me to marry a non-local girl, I asked them to introduce a local girl to me.

Both Yim and Ng admitted that their failed relationships jolted them out of their romantic fantasies and also forced them to confront their lack of breadwinning capacity and poor financial situation. They realized that relationships were not just about the romance and intimacy of two individuals engaging in an intense personal relationship; many other factors, such as a man's career prospect, his economic status, and the view of both set of parents, also shape the relationship. This is especially the case when the relationship is intended to lead to marriage. Migrating to the city had given migrant men a rosy dream of urban romance that was crushed by their relative economic inferiority. Rural-to-urban migrant men face inequalities on two fronts—they need to compete with more affluent urbanites and better-off rural counterparts. The rural-urban divide is widening in postsocialist China, but so too are economic divisions among rural people (Murphy, 2002). The failed romances of Yim and Ng reveal that rural-to-urban young migrant men's experiences of dating and romance are a class issue as well as a gender issue. While criticizing girls for being materialistic or instrumental, many young migrant men had to admit that without a wealthy family background or high earning power, they would always be undesirable mates in the urban dating game, which is largely governed by consumerism, pragmatism, and market principles. Ng's response had been to take a part-time college program, and his college degree had helped him advance his career and earn promotion to the deputy directorship of his factory. Yim had decided to focus on his work and launch his career before he continued his romantic journey.

As well as being related to their unfavorable economic position in urban areas, migrant men's difficulties on the dating scene are also related to their mobility and the instability of migrant life. Just as dating is often a part of young male migrants' experience of city romance, breakups are also an everyday experience. Many romances do not last. Migrant workers are constantly on the move between factories, cities, and regions (Choi and Peng, 2015). This mobility creates opportunities and gives them greater autonomy in employment, but it also results in more unstable romantic relationships. Chang (2008) described how easy it was for young migrants to lose contact with friends and coworkers during migration, even when they had access to advanced communication technologies. Moving apart usually leads to emotional estrangement between a couple (Farrer, 2014). Many interviewees reported that they had broken up with a girlfriend just because one party had left the place where they had met, and they had gradually lost contact. Pan, a twenty-seven-year-old cook, told us,

> I used to date a girl who was working as a waitress in the restaurant where I worked. After a while, she did not want to work as a waitress any more. So, she quit her job and found employment somewhere else. But, at that time, I was still working there. We were living in two different places. Gradually, we lost contact with each other.

Some interviewees interpreted this situation in terms of the popular Chinese discourse on predestination (*yuanfen*): they were destined to meet but were not destined to be together (*youyuan wufen*). This explanation provided a rationale for the short-term nature of their romances; it also obscured the sad fact that most migrants have a rootless existence in the city, which makes it hard, if not impossible, for them to maintain a stable, long-term relationship. Many of our interviewees did not even try to maintain long-distance relationships. In cities, one of the most radical changes in dating since the implementation of economic reforms has been "the normalization of breaking up as the end point rather than marriage" (Farrer, 2014: 77). In the social climate of urban China, where breaking up had become widely accepted as a possible end to a relationship, it was not difficult for our migrant respondents to legitimate their short-term relationships and frequent breakups. As some of them stated, "It [breaking up] is not a big deal."

PREMARITAL SEX, EXTRAMARITAL SEX, AND CONSUMPTION

The influence of Western sexual culture and the increasing social acceptance of sex for pleasure have resulted in the decoupling of sex from marriage in postreform urban China (Zhang, 2011). Sexual pleasure, like romantic passion, is now widely regarded as an essential part of intimate relationships (Jeffreys, 2006). Although rich qualitative research (Farrer, 2002; Yan, 2003; Jeffreys, 2006; Zhang, 2011) has documented the changed attitudes to sex and the sexual behaviors of young Chinese men and women—manifest in the increased prevalence of premarital sex, extra-marital sex, prostitution, and the higher consumption of pornography—there remain some differences between rural and urban attitudes to sex and sexual behavior. In urban China sex has gradually been decoupled from reproduction and marriage and normalized as an expression of romantic love, whereas in rural China sex is still largely associated with reproduction and is only regarded as acceptable within the institution of marriage (Farrer, 2014; Yan, 2003; Friedman, 2000). Premarital sex has been described as a "natural" part of urban Chinese young people's romantic relationships, but in rural China it usually has to be legitimated through an engagement ritual (Yan, 2003; Farrer, 2014). Generally speaking, urban China is more tolerant of premarital sex than rural China, although both have experienced dramatic transformations in sexual ideology and behavior since economic reforms were implemented.

Rural-to-urban migration not only exposes young migrant men to a more permissive sexual context, it also liberates them from the parental surveillance and moral code that constrain the sexual behavior of young people in rural China. As anonymous strangers in a city, young migrants may be bolder in their sexual behavior, due to the lack of outside constraints as well as feelings of loneliness and isolation (Smith and Yang, 2005). Among our young respondents, premarital sex with a partner who would not become a spouse was not uncommon, nor was patronizing sex workers unusual. As Bian told us, "Men usually do not reserve their first time [first experience of intercourse] for their wives. It is quite common that people have sex before marriage. Many of our peers visited sex workers." Mak, a security guard in his early thirties, defined himself as a playboy. Mak's work as a security guard in nightclubs in Shenzhen and Dongguan gave him more opportunities to meet girls than his counterparts working in factories and construction sites. His working environment may have affected Mak's ideas about sex and contributed to his numerous sexual encounters. Mak had dated five girls since migrating and had had casual sex with other girls he met in nightclubs. He told us:

> I was not mature. If I had been mature, I would have got married and had children. . . . I dated girls just for fun. I did not take my relationships with those girls seriously. I was like a playboy. When I needed them, I called them to come to have fun with me. When I did not need them, I did not want to see them even if they wanted to meet me. . . . I know I was pretty bad. Now, I have changed.

Mak was fairly open about his sexual adventures and did not associate sexual pleasure with commitment. His story about how he met and dated his last girlfriend is, to some extent, representative of how quickly young migrant men and women could become involved in a sexual relationship. As he told us,

> I met my last girlfriend in 2008 when she was working in a factory and I was working in a hotel. You know, factory girls are innocent and easily pursued. You talk sweetly to them and then you can easily get them. . . . At that time, one of my friends had a crush on her friend and asked for my help in pursuing the girl. I had no choice but to help him. One weekend, we met the girl that my friend fancied and she had brought a friend along with her. So, I took the other girl outside to chat and gave my friend the opportunity to spend some time alone with the girl he fancied. To give my friend enough time to chat with the girl, I tried my best to entertain her friend. . . . I said a bunch of crap, told her everything I could remember, my happy and unhappy experiences. . . . At the end, the girl thought I was pretty attractive. . . . I was the one who initiated sex, and she was not very happy at the beginning. Anyway, we did it and she became my girlfriend after that.

In this story, Mak bragged about his command of an important urban dating skill, "love talk" (*tanlianai*) (Farrer, 2014), to prove his maturity at the urban game of romance. It was also true that his skill in love talk made up for his economic deficiency when it came to attracting girls, especially, in his words, "the innocent ones." As he had confessed earlier, his slim income precluded him from practicing romance through big spending on every date, let alone in the context of a casual sexual relationship. For Mak love talk was a more feasible way of demonstrating masculine charm. Mak's frequent, casual sexual relationships with girls were not without consequences. Although Mak claimed that contraception had been used in these encounters, either through him using condoms or the girl taking contraceptive pills, he had still gotten six of them pregnant, and despite his open attitude to premarital sex Mak felt guilty about the girls who had had abortions for him. As he told us,

> I did not want to get married. So, I asked them to have abortions. If I let them give birth to the babies, that would be more troublesome and painful for both of us. Every time, I paid all the medical bills for their abortions. That is a man's responsibility. I also took care of them after their abortions. . . . Abortion damages their bodies. . . . It did not matter whether we were going to marry or not, it was my responsibility to take good care of them and make sure they had nutritious food after the abortion. Otherwise,

when they got older, they might have some disease because of the abortion. So, every time one of them had an abortion, I cooked chicken soup for them. I also bought them nourishment.

In rural China, marriage is central to definitions of manhood. As Mak was not ready to get married, or to become a father and take responsibility for looking after a family, he redefined manhood in terms of the provision of care to his many girlfriends who had abortions. Although he felt guilty about these girls because of the potential detrimental effects of abortion on their health and their bodies, he also felt that as a lover, he had fulfilled his responsibility to them by providing them with nourishing food.

In the case of married migrant men, migration sometimes increases their involvement in extramarital sex. For married men who migrate alone to the city and for migrant men whose spouse does not work in the same city, migration means prolonged separation from their spouse. The prospect of an urban adventure may motivate some married migrant men to become actively involved in dating and extramarital sex, but others may be driven by feelings of loneliness or a longing for emotional intimacy. Tsang, a thirty-two-year-old divorced carpenter, admitted to having extramarital affairs during his marriage. Migration separated him and his wife, who was working in another city, for four years. Migration also took him to different factories in the cities where he worked, and he met single young women who were not shy about expressing their sexual interest in him. Tsang eventually cohabited with one of these girls, at her request. Tsang reckoned that for his girlfriend, cohabitation was evidence of his commitment to their relationship. It was unclear whether Tsang's girlfriend was aware of the fact that Tsang was married. Tsang, however, was confident that his wife was not aware of his extramarital affair. He did not say whether his affair had contributed to the end of his marriage.

Another interviewee, Pao, a twenty-nine-year-old married man, also confessed that he had dated a girl for one month without his wife's knowledge. We asked our male respondents whether they were aware that married migrants had extramarital relationships; some reported that it was common enough for the term "temporary husband-wife relationship" (linshi fuqi) to have emerged and gain currency in the migrant community. Other informants reported that they knew that some of their migrant friends had had extramarital affairs. It is possible that it was the relative frequency of extramarital affairs in the migrant community that prompted Xinhua net, China's official online newspaper, to publish a special issue on these temporary husband-wife relationships in July 2013, arguing that the cause was the forced separation of migrant workers from their spouses for extended periods of time. The news report concluded that this was yet more evidence of the way in which the *hukou* system shackled migrant workers' families, marriages, and even sexual behavior.[3] Interestingly, although most of our male respondents denied having extramarital affairs, many of them had an ambivalent or even understanding attitude to such behavior. For example, some refrained from passing moral judgment on people who had extramarital affairs by saying that "everyone's situation is different." Others defended the practice on the grounds that "if a man is staying in the city alone and his wife or girlfriend is not with him, he needs to find a way to satisfy his needs. It is quite normal for men to do that, unless they are not normal men." To these respondents migrant men's extramarital affairs were a normal expression of masculinity. This is in line with the traditional Chinese sexual double standard: women's sexuality is strictly controlled and confined by marriage, whereas men's sexual desires and needs are regarded as "natural," making it culturally legitimate for men to seek to fulfill their sexual desires, even outside marriage (Mann, 2011).

In rural villages where everybody knows everybody else, extramarital sex is usually regarded as a corruption of public morals and is seldom tolerated. Were it not for the exorbitant cost of having a sexual liaison in the city, migration would provide rural men with ample opportunity to explore and satisfy their sexual appetites, well away from their wives or girlfriends. Tsang, the carpenter who had an affair while he was still married to his wife, broke up with his lover after one month of cohabitation, because he could no longer tolerate her extravagant spending habits. As he explained,

> She purchased cosmetics every day. Every four to five days, she purchased a pair of new shoes. I could not afford that. You know, I am not that kind of rich boss. If I did not need to support my family, I might be able to afford her consumption habits. I felt insecure when I was with her. So, I walked out of the relationship.

COMPROMISE IN ROMANCE AND COMPLYING WITH PARENTAL EXPECTATIONS

Although rural-to-urban migration shapes young migrant men's values and behavior with respect to romance and sex, it does not render them

3. http://www.xinhuanet.com/local/wgzg04.htm

totally immune to the marriage norms and family obligations that prevail in rural China. Migration has greatly widened the geographical boundaries of the dating and marriage market for rural young people and in theory translocal or transprovincial marriages should be common among migrant workers, because in the city they meet members of the opposite sex from other localities or provinces. In practice this is not the case. Fifty-three of the fifty-nine male interviewees who were married and under thirty-five years old at the time of the interview had married a local wife (i.e. a woman from the same province). Only six men married a woman from another province. Many single interviewees also indicated that they would eventually marry a local wife after they had tasted urban romance.

Rural parents generally do not want their children to marry an outsider (*wai di ren*) (i.e. someone from a different province). Zhang, a thirty-four-year-old security guard working in Shenzhen, had given up his relationship because both his and his girlfriend's parents disapproved of it. His girlfriend's parents worried that if their daughter were to marry a man from another province, or one who lived too far away from their home, they would not be able to see her regularly, and if she were to be abused, they would not know and would not be able to help:

> They [his girlfriend's parents] were worried. We were still young, only seventeen or eighteen years old. We met in the factory. . . . When I visited her parents . . . they spent the whole night trying to convince me [to give up the relationship] and in the end I told them that I would give it up. I could not force them [to approve] and I could not kidnap their daughter [laughs].

Zhang's parents objected to his relationship with an outsider, because they were worried that the girl would run away. As he explained:

> My parents are old and they follow tradition. They would not be happy if I found an outsider [*wai di ren*]. . . . They worry that outsiders might leave. . . . I am not saying that all outsider wives are not good. My sister-in-law [an outsider] and my brother are happy, but there are some [brides from another province] who run away. . . . If your wife runs away, it would be difficult to find another one unless you are really rich or powerful. If you have children, it [remarriage] is even more difficult. My parents would worry.

Migrants seem to accept that finding a local spouse is a self-protection strategy (Ma and Cheng, 2005). For women, marrying close to their natal family means that they have a protector at hand in case there is a marital or family dispute with their husband or in-laws. For men, marrying a local girl means that their family has access to more information about the girl's reputation and background. Marrying a local girl may also reduce in-law conflicts. China is a vast country, with fifty-six ethnic groups and thirty-four provincial administrative regions. Even within the Han Chinese ethnic group, people from different provinces speak different dialects and have different food preferences. Having a spouse from another province may result in family conflict because the habits and preferences of the wife are different from those of the husband and in-laws. The tension between the wife and her parents-in-law may make it a challenge for men to fulfill their traditional filial obligation to care for elderly parents. Although care of elderly parents is formally the responsibility of sons, most of the practical care is usually provided by their wives, the daughters-in-law, in rural China (Lan, 2003a). Finding a wife who is filial, can communicate with her in-laws, is willing to serve and care for them, and is well attuned to the local community is therefore crucial for men who seek to live up to traditional Chinese expectations of filial piety. For some men, marrying a local wife may also be more economical. Bian, the interviewee quoted at the beginning of this chapter, argued that marrying a local wife would allow him to save on travel expenses and the expensive gifts that in-laws in another province might expect. Finally and paradoxically, migrant men's sexual adventures in the city tend to make them suspicious of women who may also have had multiple sexual encounters during migration. Migrant men's experience of the dating practices and sexual mores of the cities does not necessarily mean that they are more liberal in their sexual attitudes than their peers who remain in the countryside. Migrant men consider premarital or extramarital sex as natural for them, but still expect their wives to be conservative in sexual matters and have less sexual experience before marriage. As Gui, a twenty-eight-year-old plumber from Guangdong, said,

> In this society, it is hard to find a girl whom you know thoroughly. I hung out in so many nightclubs and bars and met so many girls. I lost my faith in them. I will definitely not marry a girl from those nightclubs and bars. They are not marriageable. I am not saying I must marry a local girl in my home-town. I mean it is better to find a local girl whose background you know and she can communicate with my parents better.

Although migrant men may need to give up a romantic relationship they started during their migration to marry a local girl of their parents' choice, this type of marriage is nevertheless different from the traditional arranged marriage, sometimes referred to as "blind and deaf marriage" (*manghun yajia*). In a traditional arranged marriage, as practiced before

1949, grown children were not given any say in whom they married. In modern arranged marriages in rural China, as practiced by our respondents and their parents, grown children are given the opportunity to endorse or veto parental decisions. For example, parents may enlist the help of a matchmaker and shortlist a pool of acceptable candidates before asking their adult child to visit—or accompany them in visiting—all the candidates and select one. This method represents a compromise between parental authority and children's autonomy; parents have a guarantee that their child's marital partner will be acceptable to them, while the adult child has a degree of autonomy and some freedom to choose a partner. Migrant men who give up an urban romance to marry a local girl of their parents' choice are attempting to strike a balance between their longing for modern life and the pressure to fulfill traditional familial obligations. This compromise is not one that is without heartache.

CONCLUSION

Rural-to-urban migration has broadened the dating options available to both single and married rural men and given them ample opportunity to explore, experience, and experiment with romance and sex. However, rural-to-urban migration creates tensions on many levels simultaneously. Migrant men long for romance and intimacy, but their rootless lifestyle means that their relationships are often short-lived. The colorful urban city seems to offer everyone the same chance to taste modernity, yet dating is a gendered and classed game. In their enthusiastic pursuit of romance, young migrant men find themselves powerless to satisfy their girlfriends' consumption habits or unable to compete with other men at the dating game. Rather than providing a level playing field, urban dating practices constantly reminded migrant men of the gap between their earning power and the ostentatious consumer spending that is, for men, the key to success in dating relationships. Migrant men have absorbed Western ideals of love and intimacy, which emphasize mutual affection and spiritual kinship between partners. Yet eventually they find they need to give up their city lovers and return to their rural village to marry a local girl approved by their parents. These multiple tensions attest to the complex structural and interactional factors shaping migrant men's decisions about love, intimacy, and sex. Not all these decisions are driven by a desire for sexual freedom or liberation; some are taken in a bid to relieve the spiritual emptiness and loneliness of a socially and economically marginalized existence in the city, and some are a direct consequence of long-term separation from a spouse. These and other decisions reflect migrant men's liminal status: not belonging fully in either the rural or the urban milieu, caught between modern values and traditional obligations, they struggle to strike a balance between the two.

CHAPTER 4

Conjugal Power and
Diverse Strategies

Ting is a thirty-five-year-old driver who left his rural home to find work
in the city when he turned sixteen, in 1996. Ting's ideal wife would be
warm and gentle (*wenrou*) and presentable (*dafang*). He would prefer
that she not be strong and assertive (*nvqiangren*), but that she know
how to manage the household (*chijia*). On his own admission, his wife
departs from this ideal because she is "too strong" (*qiangshi*). However,
it turns out that because he became addicted to gambling when he came
to the city, he and his parents decided to find a mature and dependable
wife, who could control him (*guanzhu*) and manage the family. Thirteen years into his marriage, Ting's biggest argument with his wife had
been about whether they should build a house in his native village.
When they got married in 2001, Ting wanted to do so, considering it
essential for a man to build a house in his rural home, where the graves
of his ancestors are. His wife, however, thought it impractical to build a
house in his rural village, since the whole nuclear family was living in
the city; she wanted to buy a flat in a third place—the town near her
natal family. The argument was so intense that Ting refused to speak to
his wife for about half a month. She eventually gave in, and they built a
house in his native village in 2004. Although Ting won this battle, he is
ambivalent about his decision, because the house has been unoccupied
ever since. He and his wife had come to agree that they needed to purchase a flat in the town where her family live. Whether they will be able
to do this depends on both his and her income, and how well his wife

manages their savings. Ting's compromise with respect to his autonomy in personal spending has been to surrender most of his salary to his wife every month, keeping only few hundred yuan for his personal food and cigarette consumption .

Ting's story illustrates how traditional notions of conjugal relationships persist and the underlying tension between a woman's role as an obedient wife and her obligation to manage the household effectively. It also shows how migration to the city has brought patrilocality into question, because women may be reluctant to return to their husband's rural village, wanting instead to settle in an urban area, particularly when this means being close to their own natal family. Finally, it reveals how migrant men and women negotiate marital power and make compromises to reconcile the discrepancy between gender ideals and their actual experiences.

According to the "official model" of the Chinese family system, a daughter is a temporary member of the family, whose departure is imminent and whose value is therefore limited. On the other hand, a son "conjures up an unbroken lineage with power, property, and esteem passing in orderly and gradual fashion from generation to generation" (Stacey, 1983: 38). Croll (1994) described Chinese women's life as "transient . . . [full of] uncertainty, rupture and discontinuity" (p. 209). The widespread practice of patrilocal postmarital residence requires a woman move to live with or close to her husband's family upon marriage, and thereafter it is her husband's family rather, than her natal family, which has control over her. This is why a groom's family is required to pay a bride price to compensate the bride's family for the loss of her labor. In parts of China, some families have to "marry out" a daughter so that they can use the bride price to pay for the son's marriage, and "marry in" a daughter-in-law. Patrilocality functions as a system of exchange, with women as its currency; as Stacey (1983) argued, it is the "root structure" (p. 190) of Chinese patriarchy. Stacey (1983) further stated that the Communist Party, its rhetoric about the liberation of women notwithstanding, has never confronted this system. Selden (1993) suggested that the only Chinese Communist Party (CCP) initiative to challenge the legitimacy of patrilocality came from Jiang Qing, in a short-lived 1974–75 campaign that had very limited success. Even in that campaign, the state only encouraged intravillage marriages and the marriage of men into families with only one daughter. In spite of claims by scholars that uxorilocal marriage had been accepted by families without sons in the southeast (Wolf and Huang, 1980; Goody, 1990), it was a minority practice, and in general only men from very poor families were willing to accept the humiliation this form of marriage entailed.

Data from the 1980s and 1990s suggests that patrilocality was still widely practiced in rural China at this time. Selden (1993) found that nearly 80 percent of brides married prior to 1970 were born outside the village in which they lived as a wife; this figure was still at 55 percent for brides married between 1970 and 1984. Lavely (1991) found that in the villages of Northwest China in the 1980s the number of patrilocal marriages still greatly exceeded the number of intravillage and intracommune marriages. Judd (1994) concluded that the gender inequality that created disadvantages for women in rural China originated from the widespread practice of patrilocal postmarital residence and exogamy. These systems jointly created communities "based on one or more cores of agnatically related men" (p. 244) and excluded women from access to and management of resources, and from local leadership positions. In other words, patrilocality is a structure that renders women temporary members of their natal families and permanent outsiders in their marital families, and excludes them from access to resources and power in both.

Regarded as outsiders in both their natal and marital families, women were structurally and formally not expected to have any power within the Chinese family system. The so-called three obediences (*san cong*) codified explicitly the requirement that a woman should obey her father before marriage, her husband while married, and her son after her husband's death. However, as Hsu (1971) argued, there were multiple discrepancies between the "official model" of the Chinese family and what was common practice. Although the official model stripped women of any power in the family system, in practice women establish her authority within the family by developing emotional bonds with her children, particularly sons, and securing their loyalty towards her (Wolf, 1972). Women also used strategies such as humiliating their husband by starting a public fight, returning to their natal home, or threatening suicide as ways of gaining power in the family. A small number of women from large and wealthy families might also have been able to wield power behind the scenes as it was vividly depicted in the classic novel *The Dream of the Red Chamber*. However, the power of even these women was informal and derived from their status as wives. In a conflict between husband and wife, it was the husband who would have the final say (Stacey, 1983).

There is a dearth of recent studies of women's power in the family. Using the rather crude measure of who made decisions about gift exchange, Yan (2003) estimated that 35 percent of families in the North

China village where the fieldwork was conducted were wife-led, 19 percent were husband-led, and 46 percent were "equal-status." Studies conducted in Shanghai in 1999 suggested that in most families there was a gender specialization in decision-making, with husbands more likely to be the main decision makers in issues related to house purchase and wives the main decision makers when it came to household expenditures (Yi and Chen, 2006). In the same study, when couples were asked who was in charge of the most important family decisions, responses indicated that the husband generally had more say than the wife (Yi, 2006).

In this chapter, we first explore how rural-to-urban migration may have challenged patrilocality and shaken the foundations of peasant patriarchy. Secondly, we look at the issues rural-to-urban migration has raised with respect to marital power negotiations on three core issues: where to settle down after marriage, women's relationship with their natal families (both of which are directly related to patrilineality and patrilocality), and women's control of household expenditures. We considered household expenditures because previous studies have claimed that it is a domain in which the wife is dominant, and also because migration to cities has made marital disagreements over personal spending and household finances more frequent and intense. On the one hand, rural-to-urban migrant couples expect to pool income as members of a family. On the other hand, cities are sites of mass consumption, and migrant men often cannot resist consumption temptations. Although migrant men generally recognize the legitimacy of the wife's role as the household manager and her control over their and the family's finances, they devise strategies to resist wifely control over their smoking, drinking, gambling, and visits to bars and massage parlors.

PATRIARCHY AND ITS CONTRADICTIONS

Nearly all of our married respondents with sons told us that they endured the bitterness and loneliness of *dagong* life in the city in order to save enough money to build a house. The house was not for them personally, but for their son on his marriage. In contrast, single respondents could spend their money freely if their parents had paid to build a house for them. The few single respondents who did not already have a house waiting for them when they married did not seem particularly worried; they firmly believed that their fathers would have a house built for them in time. All migrant men complained that house prices were increasing rapidly. They were also disgruntled that women nowadays were so pragmatic, and that men without a house had no chance of finding a marital partner. The term "naked marriage" (luohun) was coined to describe men who succeeded in getting married despite not having a house. Sons are charged with the "noble mission" of continuing the family name and line, so getting married and establishing a family (chengjia lishi) is not seen as a matter of personal choice by rural migrants, but as an obligation toward one's family. And just as sons have an obligation to get married, parents, particularly fathers, have a corresponding duty to make sure that their sons have what is deemed necessary for an honorable marriage. In rural China this parental responsibility includes building and furnishing a house, paying the bride price, and paying for the wedding banquets. Our respondents estimated that the total budget for a marriage could easily amount to half a million yuan for a man: two hundred to three hundred thousand yuan to build a house and furnish it, and another two hundred thousand yuan for the wedding itself. Given that the median income of our respondents was between three thousand and 3999 yuan per month, it would take the typical migrant man more than ten years to save for a son's wedding, even if he did not spend a single yuan of his wages. Although relatives usually lend money to each other for house building and marriage preparations, the parents are expected to repay the debt. It is not unusual for a migrant man in his fifties still to be working to repay debts incurred for his son's marriage.

In view of the heavy financial burden a son's marriage places on his parents, parents who had already built houses for their sons regarded themselves as lucky, because prices had risen so much in recent years. The financial burden is particularly hard for migrant men with more than one son. The fourteen migrant men among our respondents who only had daughters congratulated themselves that they did not have to worry about building extra houses. Single migrant men struggled to reconcile their personal fondness for daughters with the familial obligation to bear sons.

Here is where we find the first contradiction in the Chinese patriarchy. Sons are charged with the central role of continuing the family line, and because of this parents are obliged to fund their marriage. This imposes great financial pressure on families and has resulted in the younger generation of men gradually coming to prefer daughters over sons. However, while daughters may be economically favored, they have remained inferior in the patriarchal family structure. Peasants prefer sons not because they want to, but because they are obliged to. There was a deep-seated feeling that not to ensure one's posterity was the gravest of the three most unfilial acts (the other two unfilial acts are not to take care of aged parents and not to correct parents' mistakes); this idea still resonated strongly for our respondents. For example, we met a childless migrant man who had spent all his savings from *dagong* trying to find a cure for his infertility. The obligation to have sons gives rise to another contradiction insofar as it results in an imbalance in sex ratios (Murphy, Tao, and Lu, 2011) that leads to women being favored by the marriage market. The strong obligation on sons to marry further strengthens women's bargaining power in marriage negotiations. Women, the "unnecessary" offspring, end up having more bargaining power in the marriage market because of their relative scarcity, and they use this power to negotiate for a marital residence close to their own rather than their husband's family.

At another level, although Chinese women are required to obey their father, husband, and son at different stages of their life, all our respondents defined femininity as based on a woman's ability to manage the household. Many went so far as to consider it a woman's duty to control (*guan*) her husband. This discrepancy may reflect changes in gender norms between ancient and postsocialist China. It may also reflect class variation in the role of women, with Confucian teaching on women's subordinate position in the family followed zealously chiefly by the upper class. It may also be that previous studies have attributed too submissive and stereotypical a role to Chinese women. Nonetheless, it appears that there are several layers of internal contradiction in male notions of "virtuous wifehood." While peasant men value the qualities of a capable household manager in a wife, they also demand that she show a certain obedience and deference, and they expect her always to put them and their family's interests before herself and her family. They hold firmly onto their role as the head of the household. As Wong, a twenty-six-year-old factory worker from Henan, asserted,

> Women marry into men's families. Men are in charge, right? . . . She [a wife] needs to be a reasonable person. She needs to know when to give you face (*mian zi*, meaning show respect).

Pao, a twenty-nine-year-old electrician from rural Guangdong, held similar views:

> Modern society goes for gender equality. Women can have their own careers. But all men love warm and tender women who listen to them.

Ting, the thirty-five-year-old driver from rural Guangdong whose story we discussed at the beginning of this chapter, further elaborated:

Men need a wife who can manage the household. She can have a job. She does not need to be beautiful, but she needs to know the appropriate manner [*da fang*].

& pressure

Here we see another contradiction inherent in Chinese patriarchy: a wife is expected to "control" her husband and manage "his" household, yet at the same time she is required to be gentle and deferential. She is therefore faced with the delicate balancing act of exercising her power while remaining within certain implicit bounds that uphold traditional ideas about male dominance. She should never cause her husband to lose face or openly challenge his role as head of the household and primary provider. She should also know when and how to defer to him and preserve his apparent dominance. Most men value the notion of family harmony highly; this translates into having a wife who will not "talk back and create conflict" (*dachao danao*), who defers to her husband (*rangyidian*) when the couple disagree, and who puts up with his bad temper (*renyixia*). How do these contradictions play out in marital power negotiations between migrant men and their wives?

MIGRATION AND THE NEW CONTEXT FOR MARITAL POWER NEGOTIATION

Migration creates new tension for marital power negotiation, because migrant men and women differ significantly regarding their intention to return to the rural area of their origin (Zhu, 2007; Zhu and Chen, 2010). Migrant men generally viewed their sojourn in the city as temporary and purely instrumental. Ruan, a twenty-seven-year-old restaurant owner from Hunan, explained:

> I am in the city to earn money. I am not going to settle down here . . . when I have saved enough money, I will definitely be going home. . . . Like fallen leaves settling back to their roots [*luo ye gui gen*] . . . I am definitely going back home. . . . For a start, I don't have many relatives in the city. Secondly I am a traditional person who likes that feeling of being at home in the village. Thirdly, property prices are so high in the city and the financial pressure is huge. Not to mention that the locals discriminate against us. . . . I stay in the city to make money and I will definitely be leaving. When the time comes I am going home. . . . The village has this human touch . . . my neighbors, my childhood friends, my memories and feelings. My village is not as well off as the cities, but there is trust . . . you can open your heart to people. Outside [in the city], you meet different people and you hide away and do not have much social life.

Migrant men associated their village with their good memories of childhood and carefree adolescence, with mutual family support, and with a sense of community among neighbors. On the other hand, the city puts pressure on them, they blame it for their frustrations, and it makes them isolated. The *hukou* system, which excludes migrant workers from full citizenship and denies their children access to public education, increases male migrant workers' feeling that they will forever be outsiders in the city, and that urban residents discriminate against them. Specifically, male migrant workers contrasted the isolation of city life and the alienation they felt in the city with the flamboyance, human warmth, and feeling of acceptance in their native communities. Pan, a twenty-seven-year-old cook from Hunan, told us,

> I will go back and build a house in my native village. I am not willing to buy a flat in the urban area . . . it feels more like home in the village. Neighbors visit each other and play games together. It feels good. You can visit this relative today, and visit another one tomorrow. It feels friendly. In the urban area this is impossible. Sometimes you can't even have a word with your next-door neighbour in the urban area.

However, a male migrant worker's fondness for and unrelenting loyalty to his native village stands in sharp contrast to his wife's aspiration to settle in urban areas or live close to her family, particularly if her family is living in a town. Women cited as factors in their desire to settle in urban areas or to live close to their natal family after marriage: the help their parents could provide with child care, the convenience of having amenities close by and access to transport systems, the cleanliness of urban dwellings and the urban environment, and most importantly, the chance of paid employment and the independent income this would give them.

In addition to gender difference in settlement intention among the migrant population, migration has also made marital negotiation over finances more intense. Migration to the city allows migrant men to earn a larger income, but has simultaneously increased the frequency and stake of marital negotiation over finances. Cities are sites for mass consumption, and temptations to spend hard-earned cash are omnipresent. Couples may disagree about what to buy and how much to spend. Migrant men who are absentee fathers often try to compensate their left-behind children by lavishing on them expensive items of clothing, toys, and tasty snacks when they do see them. Pragmatic wives tend to be more concerned about saving money and may disapprove of their husband's generosity or criticize him for spoiling the children. Many men also confessed that their wives objected to their gambling, drinking, and smoking, since all these habits cost money. However, smoking, drinking, and gambling are part of a male migrant worker's social life, things they do when they are with their mates, and cutting the budget for these activities effectively means cutting their social ties. Several men also said that men want to gain the approval of their peers, and so they spend money on their friends, e.g. paying for a dinner; this may also trigger marital discord. Men's fondness for gadgets and mobile phones tends not to go down well with their wives, who often consider such trendy consumer items a waste of money. The most frequent trigger for marital conflict seemed to be a husband's gambling problem. Data from our questionnaire showed that of the 189 male respondents who answered questions on gambling, one respondent (0.9 percent) reported gambling every day, 6.9 percent once or twice every week, 11.1 percent several times a month, and 19.6 percent several times a year. Respondents may have underreported their gambling; one respondent complained that the questionnaire item was too general, and that occasionally playing cards or mah-jong should not be counted as gambling. Seven respondents admitted in in-depth interviews that they used to be, or still were, addicted to gambling. We also heard about two divorces caused by the husband's gambling addiction. Although gambling is common among rural men in the agricultural off-season (Hsu, 1971), male migrant workers in cities tend to gamble with coethnics to forget their boredom, loneliness, and the monotony of their work lives. One man regretted his decision to make a career as a security guard. He complained that the work was so uninteresting and unchallenging that it had led him and many of his coworkers to turn to heavy gambling for excitement and some sense of meaning. Migrant men may begin by playing cards with coethnics on days off, and end up visiting underground gambling dens every day after work. Gambling not only costs some migrant men their relationship, it may also cost them their livelihood. One respondent told us that he lost his taxi through gambling. Some male migrant workers work hard in the city, but when they return home for an extended visit during one of the festivals, they try to make up for the bitterness of their *dagong* life by gambling, and end up losing their hard-earned cash to villagers. One male migrant worker reported that during the period when he was gambling heavily, he did not leave the village to return to work in the city for many months. Gambling is thus a part of male migrant workers' social life, used by some as an escape from the monotony and loneliness of city *dagong* life; it punctuates their mobility between rural and urban milieus.

If women struggle to control their migrant husbands' gambling, they are even more powerless when it comes to his visits to karaoke bars and massage parlors. Many wives disapprove of such visits not just because they are expensive, but because they fear their husbands will have affairs with the women working there. However, if a woman remains in the village while her husband is working in the city, she often lacks information and the means to control his visits to these entertainment venues. Although only two migrant men (Tsang, a thirty-two-year-old carpenter, and Pao, a twenty-nine-year-old electrician) in our sample admitted to having had an extramarital affair during their migrant life, many respondents reported knowing at least one male migrant worker who had "created a mess outside" (*zaiwaimian luanlai;* meaning to have an extramarital affair) because of the long separations from his wife. Fear that their husbands will have affairs if they stay in the city alone is one of the factors that has encouraged women to leave the village and migrate to the city. Our quantitative data also confirmed that the migrant couple working in the same city is a rather common form of relationship; around 59 percent of our married male respondents (81) had a spouse working in the same city.

BIG DECISIONS, SMALL DECISIONS

In the first five field trips in 2012 and 2013,[1] we asked 115 male in-depth interviewees to complete a short questionnaire that included questions on how they viewed the statement that "the man is the head of the household, the person who makes the most important decisions for the family." The percentages of migrant men answering "definitely disagree," "disagree," "neither agree nor disagree," "agree," and "definitely agree" were 3.5, 19.3, 23.7, 40.4 and 12.3 percent, respectively. Those who chose the option "neither agree nor disagree" explained that they felt couples should discuss issues, try to reach consensus, and make joint decisions. These results demonstrated that over half (52.7 percent) of these 115 male respondents endorsed the traditional norm: a male

1. Upon completing each in-depth interview, we asked the interviewee to fill in a questionnaire that provided information on his/her demographic background and attitude toward certain issues. The questionnaire used in the first five field trips was slightly different from the one used in the subsequent field trips.

head of the household and male dominance in marriage. Given the many discrepancies between the official model of the Chinese family system and reports of what is customary in practice, in the same questionnaire we asked our respondents whether it was true that most decisions in their family "were made by their wife or made jointly by the couple"; the percentages of migrant men answering "definitely not true," "not true," "neither true nor false," "true," and "definitely true" were 1.8, 21.5, 34.2, 31.6, and 7 percent, respectively, indicating that in practice only 23.2 percent of men were dominant decision makers in their family. How can we explain the discrepancy between our respondents' endorsement of the official model of male dominance and how their relationships operated in practice, i.e. joint decision making or wife-dominated decision making? Our in-depth interview data suggested that migrant men distinguished between big and small decisions and insisted on having the final say in big decisions. Ma, an eighteen-year-old hotel service worker from rural Guangdong, summed it up:

Small decisions, women can make; big decisions have to be made by men.

"Big decisions" are those related to three issues: 1) Where should the couple eventually settle down—near the husband's family or the wife's? 2) To which family does the wife owe the greatest loyalty—her natal family or her husband's family? 3) Should the wife remain in the city or return to the village to look after the young and the old? "Small decisions" are mostly related to household finances and the husband's spending.

UNCOMPROMISING BIG DECISIONS: PATRILINEALITY AND PATRILOCALITY

Male migrant workers are unlikely to compromise on the first two of the "big decisions" listed above, since they are central to the norms of patrilineality and patrilocality that underlie the patriarchal Chinese family system. Tang, a thirty-one-year-old single shoemaker, split up with his girlfriend (whom he met after migration) because her family wanted an uxorilocal marriage. The arrangements for an uxorilocal marriage vary according to the prenuptial contract, but usually the man has to live with his wife's family and let his children take his wife's surname. Tang rejected uxorilocal marriage primarily because of what he referred to as "male dignity" (nanren de zunyan), the status of men in the family and community and the symbolic boundaries of respectable manhood:

Her family does not have sons. So her parents wanted me to marry into their family. That is impossible no matter how rich her family is. . . . People would look down on me. Wherever I went, I would be considered inferior. . . . Her parents would always look down on me. There would not be a place for me. What I said would never count. And whatever I did, I would need their approval. . . . Maybe some people would think that it does not matter that I marry into her family because they have money. But not for me!

Lu, a twenty-six-year-old migrant worker had also split up with his girlfriend of three years for the same reason. Lu and his ex-girlfriend, both migrant workers, met in 2006 in Dongguan. At first her parents complained that his family was too far away. Later, when they agreed to let her marry him, they asked him to marry into their family and let the children use her surname, conditions which would have made it in essence an uxorilocal marriage. Lu agreed to the arrangement, but his parents opposed it, because they considered it a disgrace for the family.

In addition to uxorilocal marriage, how married women divide their loyalty after marriage has increasingly become a contentious issue for migrant men. Culturally women were not expected to financially support their parents after marriage, and women in rural areas had no independent income to do so even if they wanted to. However, now that many rural women have access to paid employment in urban areas, they have the financial resources to do so. Migrant women from families with no sons are particularly likely to perceive their continued support of their natal family after marriage to be both legitimate and necessary. Migrant men, however, may object to this practice. Tsang's marriage—he was a thirty-two-year-old carpenter from Hubei province—ended in divorce, because of his dissatisfaction with the continued loyalty of his wife (also a migrant worker) to her natal family and the financial support she gave her parents after their marriage. He thought that women should follow their husbands after marriage, just as the old Chinese saying has it:

People say, "Marry a chicken, follow the chicken; marry a dog, follow the dog; and marry a monkey, follow him all around the mountain." . . . If she wants to listen to her father's advice, I'm not complaining, it just means we cannot be together anymore.

Most migrant men also reject the idea of moving to live with or close to their wife's family after marriage. Wu, a thirty-eight-year-old construction worker, ended his first marriage because his wife insisted that they live close to her family:

Her mother is in Guangzhou. . . . After we got married, we went to work in Guangzhou. First her mother wanted to move her [his first wife's] *hukou* [from my village] to Guangzhou. . . . Then she [his first wife] said she would not go back to my native village. She wanted to buy a flat in Guangzhou. . . . She was very close to her mother and her mother had got married again, to a man in Guangzhou. . . . Divorce is rare in my village. It was a big decision for me because it was going to be difficult for me to find another wife after the divorce.

Despite recognizing that a divorce would have a negative effect on his reputation, Wu had still been unwilling to compromise on patrilocality. When male migrant workers compromised on this issue, they faced tremendous pressure from their parents and extended family. They are considered traitors to the Chinese family system. Zhang, a thirty-four-year-old security guard from Henan province, complained that his brother was like "a daughter who has married out," because after marrying he had moved to live with his wife's family in Hubei province:

> They moved to live in Hubei. Their child was born and raised in Hubei. . . . Even the house was built in Hubei. He has no plans to return to our native village. Although my father has two sons, my brother is like a daughter who has married out. Now I am the only son left. . . . Two brothers, but now there is only one [son].

Zhang was proud that he had fulfilled his duty as a son to support his parents in their old age; he looked after the family's land and house. Underlying his pride, however, was the sense of loss and betrayal he felt toward his brother, because of his brother's decision to go against the custom of patrilocality. It is not that migrant men want to cut their wife off from her natal family—Zhang, for instance, has maintained a close relationship with his wife's family. It is rather that they expect the wife's family to take second place and that the couple owe the husband's family the greater loyalty. For example, when migrant workers visit family for a festival, the official day of the festival is usually reserved for the husband's family, with a visit to the wife's family either before or after the day of celebration. Wong, a twenty-six-year-old married male migrant worker, explained the delicate arrangements:

> For the Chinese New Year, we visit her [his wife's] family first, we go there a few days before Chinese New Year's Day. It is an obligation for a son-in-law to visit his parents-in-law. . . . It takes some organization. . . . After that, we go back to my parents' home to celebrate the Chinese New Year. . . . Across the whole of China, women marry into men's families, the man's family takes priority, right?

COMPROMISE ON A BIG DECISION: WIFE LEAVING THE VILLAGE FOR WORK IN THE CITY

In our questionnaire of the 115 male migrants interviewed in the course of the first five field trips we asked if they agreed with the statement that "a man's main responsibility is to provide for his family." The percentages of respondents who answered "definitely disagree," "disagree," "neither agree nor disagree," "agree," and "definitely agree" were 0, 8.8, 9.6, 48.2, and 30.7, respectively. These results indicate that the great majority (almost 80 percent) of the 115 male respondents defined manhood predominantly in terms of being a provider. If the man is the main provider, then it follows that the woman, even if the couple has migrated to the city, will be the main family carer and will need to return to the village to assume this role when her services are needed. Jiang, a thirty-four-year-old construction worker from Henan, stated matter-of-factly,

> Of course my woman has to return to care for the children. Primary and secondary school years are the critical times for children.

Around 42 percent (57) of our 137 married respondents were individual migrants. Many of this group were married men who had left their wives behind to take care of children and elderly parents. For example Chan, a fifty-year-old construction worker from Hunan province, has always worked in the city, whereas his wife stayed at home doing farm work and looking after their four children until their youngest son was eighteen years old. Thereafter she joined Chan in the city and found herself a factory job. Chan is adamant that men should leave home and work in the city to support their family while the wife stays at home to take care of the children. In his words, "It is uselessness if people only think about earning money and leave their children uncared for."

However, increasingly the wives of migrant men are reluctant to fulfil what their husband considers their "natural" role, simply because they prefer paid employment in the city to being a caregiver in the village. Tong's wife, a twenty-five-year-old female migrant worker from Sichuan province, had left her son in her mother-in-law's care when he was three months old. She simply did not like looking after babies and preferred paid factory employment in the city. Although Tong initially opposed his wife's decision to leave their son behind , his mother supported her because of the financial benefits her city job would have for the family. Zhou, a twenty-six-year-old taxi driver, explained why he gave in when his wife insisted on leaving their son with his grandfather and came to work in the city:

Of course, she likes working in the city. How much can one person earn? When you don't have money for rent or when the milk powder is finished, you really don't know what to do. If my grandfather can look after our children, she should definitely work. For us rural migrant workers, when our children are born, the only thing that matters is how we can earn money to support them, and pay for their education. . . . There are no other options.

So while the male provider role is a defining element of peasant worker masculinity, and these men would like their wives to stay in the village to care for their children, many have compromised on this issue because of financial pressure.

NEGOTIATING SMALL DECISIONS: FOUR PATTERNS

As discussed above, migrant men distinguished between big and small decisions, and claimed that they left the small decisions to their wives. This is consistent with their belief that a wife should control her husband and manage the household. Ma, an eighteen-year-old male migrant worker, explained:

It is the norm in rural areas that men should get married early. The wife can control him and ensure that he listens to her. She needs to put him in his place [zhenzhu], turn him into a more grounded person, not someone who only cares about having fun.

In spite of the general expectation that the wife control her husband and be in charge of household expenditures, conjugal disagreements over money, particularly migrant men's personal spending, are common. In the following, we identified four patterns of marital negotiation over migrant men's spending: delegation, communication, ostensible concession, and confrontation.

Delegation

Delegation refers to husbands who transfer decision-making power to their wives but retain the power of veto. This is the strategy closest to the official model, in which the wife is in charge of household finances and is given the right to control the husband's money. Migrant men adopting this model may hand their whole wage over to their wives and ask for spending money when they need it. If the wife lives back in the village, the man will keep a small proportion of his wages to cover day-to-day expenses and send the rest home to her. Most of these men have considerable trust and confidence in their wives' personality and financial management. Chan, a fifty-year-old construction worker, told us proudly,

> All my money is in the hands of my old woman. I haven't got a yuan . . . it is all in her name. I don't know any of the details. . . . I know that she will not spend the money improperly. She knows what she should do, I would not try to control her.

Some men explained that this practice was in accordance with the village norm, while others simply allowed it, because otherwise they would just spend all their money, as Lau, a thirty-two-year-old shop owner from Henan province, confessed:

> If I control my money, I spend it all. I spend it on drinking, dining out, going to karaoke bars, and massage parlors. I like to pay for my friends when we dine out. I like to have foot massages, and I gamble it all away, and . . . you know . . . occasionally on women [other than his wife].

Communication

Communication is characterized by discussion between the husband and wife before decisions are made. This strategy stresses the need to communicate, discuss, and reach a consensus. Fung, a twenty-six-year-old factory worker from Jiangxi, for instance, said that he and his wife, who is also a migrant worker in the same city, "consult each other" and "discuss things." Migrant men who adopt this strategy say that they have equal power with their spouse. To ensure that power is exercised based on consensus, they establish mechanisms to prevent either of the two parties from spending money before a consensus is reached. When Deng, a twenty-six-year-old migrant worker from Hunan province, could not agree with his wife on whether he should use his savings to start a small business, the couple decided that while Deng would keep his savings in his bank account, his wife would keep the bank card of his account. That way he would not be able to spend his money without her knowledge and agreement:

> I want to start a small business. . . . She worried that we would lose the money. I told her that we could not worry too much. If we worry too much, we can only *dagong* all our life. . . . The money is in my account, but she has the bank card.

Migrant men who adopt this strategy usually consider their wives' contribution, either through her income or her important services to the family. Jin, a forty-one-year-old migrant worker from rural Guangdong, insisted that he needed to consult his wife on important decisions because this was "reasonable" and "equal." Jin's wife stayed at their rural home to look after their two teenage children:

> She is filial to my parents. She educates the children well. She does not work (paid employment). But I think her work for the family is more important than mine. My whole family depends on her. I am only earning some money. . . . I do not have the ability to look after the whole family.

Jin viewed the work that his wife did for the family as real work, did not devalue her contribution because she did not hold paid employment, and regarded the family as the most crucial aspect of a man's life. The emphasis on the centrality of family happiness led him to conclude that his wife's role in the family has made her a key player in its decision-making process.

Ostensible Concession

Ostensible concession refers to husbands making small compromises and paying lip service to their wife's requests but then disregarding them behind her back. Migrant men adopting this pattern of negotiation devise various strategies, including making small concessions, pretending to acknowledge their wife's opinion, or hiding their spending from her. For example, despite his wife's opposition Lam, a twenty-year-old migrant worker from Sichuan province, did not have any intention of quitting smoking, drinking, and gambling because he could not imagine a social life with his mates which did not involve these three activities. He tried to reduce his cigarette consumption by avoiding smoking inside the house or in front of his wife, and to decrease the extent of his gambling:

> I used to be a heavy smoker. Now my wife is pregnant, I smoke less at home . . . a little bit less . . . but it is difficult for a man not to smoke. The smoking provides a context for conversation. Men start to talk when they smoke and exchange cigarettes. I pass them one and they pass me one. . . . If I am not smoking I cannot accept their cigarette when they pass it to me. It feels awkward. Drinking is the same. Smoking and drinking, most men cannot do without these two. . . . Gambling sometimes, I get bored if I do not gamble, but I make small bets, one- or two-yuan bets.

Lam said that his wife seemed to be satisfied for the moment with the small concessions that he has made. One wonders what will happen when their child is born, and the family is under greater financial pressure. Sun, a forty-one-year-old taxi driver, often paid lip service to his wife's complaints about the amount of time he spends socializing with his friends and the money he spends drinking and dining out with them:

> You see there are many coethnics here. Sometimes I stay out with them until very late at night. When she calls [I answer the phone and tell her I am coming home soon], but I don't actually go home soon. She is often mad at me and will ignore me for days, but afterwards life just goes on.

Lau, a thirty-two-year-old shop owner from Henan province, hid his gambling and the resulting debt from his wife:

> I still owe my friends several thousand yuan—money I lost in the gambling. I have to return it slowly. . . . Of course my wife does not know [about his debt].

Confrontation

Confrontation is characterized by the husband using violence to silence his wife when she complains about his spending, rather than negotiating his personal spending options with her. Tam, a thirty-five-year-old factory worker from Guizhou, was the primary provider for her family, because her husband used to have gambling problems. Tam and her husband were introduced to us at the same time. They were interviewed separately by two interviewers, and both interviews revealed a history of intimate partner violence. When we talked to Tam, she gave us her history of spousal violence and victimization:

> If he had just been playing cards once in a while, for relaxation, I would have been fine with it. But he gambled every day, and ignored the kids, and when I complained he hit me.

When we interviewed Tam's husband, he did not deny using physical violence against his wife, but defended his actions by saying,

> My wife is very strict with me. Like gambling, it is a no and no. She would tell me not to go [gambling] and she would go on and on, I can totally imagine what she used to say.

Suen, a thirty-four-year-old factory worker from Henan province, told us that he used physical force against his wife when they fought about money:

> It is all about money. Our fights. She said I should not spend money so freely. . . . Men all love to have face and if I dine out with friends, sometimes

I pay for them and sometimes they pay for me. . . . Sometimes it is the gadgets that I have bought. She thought that these were unnecessary purchases. She is very frugal and careful about money.

Suen was earning three to four thousand yuan per month. His wife earned more than he did because of overtime work. Suen found it difficult to accept that he was the "lesser person" in the relationship:

Sometimes I ask myself why as a man I am earning less than a woman. I question myself every day. Every day. Why is she earning more than me? Of course it is difficult to accept. As a man I am supposed to support the family. In the end, I could not support them. In the end, it is my wife who is making the most money.

Suen's use of physical violence to silence his wife's complaints about his spending may be a tactic to restore his sense of masculinity. His wife's higher income appears to have created a status conflict and a crisis in his identity as a man. Rural-to-urban migration has provided peasant women with unprecedented opportunities to gain financial independence. In many instances migrant women are able to earn more money than their migrant husbands because of the availability of overtime work in factories.

CONCLUSION

This chapter outlines the complex dynamics of marital power negotiation resulting from and related to migration, the continuities as well as changes to the traditional pattern of male dominance within a marriage. It also discusses how migration has created new tensions for marital power negotiation. Our analysis shows that many migrant men distinguish between big and small decisions. They strive to preserve their dominance when it comes to big decisions related to patrilineality and patrilocality, although they are forced to make compromises in some instances. For example, most men considered unquestionable the norm that men work and women are caretakers. However, often financial pressures had made them compromise and withdraw their objections when their wife decided to leave her role as carer for family members and migrate to the city to find work. While Chinese women are expected to be household managers and control their husbands' finances, they are also expected to be obedient and deferential, which makes marital power negotiations delicate and contentious. We have identified four patterns of marital negotiation of household finances: delegation, communication, ostensible concession, and confrontation. Delegation is the strategy closest to the traditional practice of a man allowing his wife to manage his finances. Older men who were confident of their wife's personality and ability as a financial manager were most likely to adopt this pattern. In couples adopting the communication strategy, finances of the household and the husband were managed through discussion and consensus or joint decision making. Men who valued their wives' contributions to the family, either through paid employment or unpaid housework and child-care services, were the most likely to negotiate finances in this way. Ostensible concession is the term we have used to characterize men who made small concessions and paid lip service to their wife's demands while acting differently behind her back. Finally, we described relationships in which confrontation replaced negotiation, and the husband used physical violence to silence his wife's complaints about his spending habits. Migrant men who had a gambling problem or earned less than their wives seemed to be most likely to adopt this approach. To them violence was not simply a way of silencing a disagreeing wife, but a means of restoring their sense of manhood in a reversed-status relationship.

These diverse responses highlight the variability in approaches to marital power negotiations that results from or is related to migration, the contentious nature of the negotiation process, the contradictions between the official family model and what happens in practice, and the discrepancies between the normative gender ideals of migrant men and the socioeconomic reality for migrant families.

CHAPTER 5

Housework and Respectability

Ting, the thirty-five-year-old migrant whose experience we discussed at the beginning of chapter 4, worked as a driver for a company in Dongguan, and his wife worked as an account clerk in the same city when we met him in 2012. They had two children, aged twelve and six. Although Ting and his wife both worked in Dongguan, he lived in the dormitory provided by his employer, and his wife lived with their two children in a rented apartment in another part of the city. As he only stayed for the weekends, returning home on Friday night, he could not help look after their children during the week. This had caused major arguments. Ting apparently endorsed the traditional "male outside, female inside" (*nanzhuwai, nvzhunei*) cultural norm. He explained that his wife managed their household, whereas he tended to tasks outside the home or physically demanding chores. However, he was also aware of the discrepancies between his ideal of family life and the reality. His wife's salary (which was higher than his) was critical to the family's economic stability: it was needed to pay school fees for their two children, who did not have *hukou* in the city and therefore had to study at private schools charging around five thousand yuan a year per student. Recognition of the importance of his wife's contribution as a breadwinner had only produced limited change in his behavior; he refused to move back to live with his wife and children, and often found excuses to avoid domestic chores such as mopping and sweeping the floor, washing dishes, and cleaning the bathroom. He did, however, "help out" with cooking, supervising their children's homework, and taking them to the doctor when he was at home.

The situation of Ting and his family highlights the pressing demands on dual-earner migrant households in the city with children. Although the majority of early cohorts of married migrants left their children in the countryside, there is evidence that the number of family migrants is increasing. In our sample, thirty men had migrated with their spouse and children. Away from the village, these families usually lack access to extended family support. Unable to afford paid child care, these migrant couples have to renegotiate domestic chores and child care so that they can combine work and family responsibilities. The financial pressure on these migrants is intense; the cities deny them full citizenship and their children access to public education (see chapter 2 for more detailed discussion). This makes the wife's participation in paid employment an economic necessity, and shouldering some responsibility for child care and domestic chores becomes an unavoidable obligation for migrant men.

Like men who migrate with their families, men who migrate as part of a couple also need to renegotiate domestic chores, both in the city and in between the city and their rural home. Fifty-one of our respondents had migrated as part of a couple. In these families, the wife typically holds down a factory job requiring long hours of overtime, which makes her unavailable for domestic chores. Many of these migrant couples had left their young children, some as young as one or two years old, in the countryside under the care of grandparents. One of the partners has to return to the rural village frequently, to see the children, take care of sick elderly parents, or deal with other family issues. Given the entrenched ideology of "men outside, women inside" and the general exemption of rural men from domestic chores, how do migrant men face the new reality and renegotiate their participation in domestic chores after migration?

The official model of the Chinese patriarchy was built on a rigid segregation of the sexes, which reserved the outside, public domain exclusively for men, and confined women to the inside, the domestic sphere (Mann, 2011). The cosmological dualism of yang and yin, and the cultural claim that men and women are intrinsically different (*nannu youbie*), were used jointly to legitimize the separation of the sexes and the seclusion of women. This gender order was viewed as parallel when in fact it was fundamentally hierarchical. Its enforcement ensured the exclusion of women from access to economic resources, political power, and social status; it rendered their dependence on the family complete and made them totally subject to the control of the patriarch. In practice, sex segregation was far from complete in ordinary peasant households (Ebrey, 1993); economic necessity meant that women in these households were often required to participate in household subsistence activities (e.g. weaving, spinning, raising livestock, etc.) and small-scale trading, which allowed them to venture outside the house (Hsu, 1971; Gilmartin et al., 1994). However, these local deviations did not affect the identity of women, which was still based on their domestic role and responsibilities; it only meant that women in peasant households had many more responsibilities than men. In an ethnographic study of a rural market town in the early 1940s, Hsu (1971) observed that "in general women work much harder than do men. Women usually get up fairly early in the morning, work like beasts of burden throughout the day, and go to bed fairly early in the evening; while the men get up very late in the morning, talk and drink tea and/or smoke opium throughout the better part of the day, and go to bed much later than their wives and mothers" (p. 72). In spite of their role in household production and their essential contribution to its survival, women in peasant households remained the inferior, "inside" person (Stacey, 1983).

When the Communists came to power in 1949, one of their main policies was to encourage women to participate in production (Croll, 1974). Women were called, mobilized, and eventually required to participate fully in the work of the communes to collect work points for their household. However, women's increased participation in production did not result in a reduction in their domestic duties, nor did it dramatically change the gender division of housework. When the Communist state wanted to maximize the productive labor of women in the 1950s, rather than advocate an equal division of domestic chores between men and women, community services such as crèches, nurseries, grain-grinding centers, sewing centers, and dining facilities were set up to reduce the number of household chores. In many areas the socialization of household labor proved short-lived; facilities were closed down because of unsatisfactory standards or exorbitant costs, and since then, in rural China, household chores have generally been shared among the women in a household. For example, older women may retire from production activities to take responsibility for the domestic chores and take care of young children, while younger women participate in remunerative work during day and care for their children and do chores at night.

Two surveys conducted in 1980 showed that both in urban and rural China, women performed the majority of the domestic work (Croll, 1983). Ironically, the liberation of women by the Communists only piled additional responsibilities—for production and remunerative activities—on the shoulders of peasant women who were already doing the bulk of sideline activities and domestic chores (Croll, 1981). Peasant women worked alongside men in the communes; they also grew vegetables in their courtyard gardens, raised livestock, and gathered fuel for the household. Their other domestic duties included processing farm produce for consumption (e.g. grinding corn and preserving vegetables), sewing, cooking, and child care. Peasant women's heavy work load led Croll (1981) to argue that the survival of peasant households was dependent on peasant women's self-exploitation.

When conducting fieldwork in three villages in Northern China in the late 1980s Judd (1994) noticed that rural men found the idea that they might share domestic chores unimaginable, even laughable. In a study of another northern village in the late 1990s, Yan (2003) found that "in most families it is still the wife who does the household chores" (p. 97). In rural China, in terms of the gendered division of domestic labor, the revolution was postponed (Wolf, 1985). In an analysis of this "postponed revolution" Croll (1983) suggested that although the Communist state advocated gender equality, its views on housework and child care were inconsistent. Although state media reiterated that housework was an important part of shared married life, and advised husbands to help their wives in order to maintain marital harmony, the discourse was not one of equality (Croll, 1974). Many chores (e.g. looking after children and sewing) were still considered "feminine activities" and were therefore the woman's job (Croll, 1985). More importantly, domestic work was conceived by the state as "'extraneous worries' outside of the mainstream of social, political and economic life" (Croll, 1983, p. 68). Gender equality in the division of domestic chores and child care was viewed by the Communist Party as a trivial matter, of secondary status in the grand narrative of modernization and national strength. Furthermore, state propaganda often placed conflicting demands on women; they were encouraged to prioritize their work over their domestic chores, while at the same being urged to "invest more time and energy in their mothering roles, invest in familial relations and be guardians of socialist morality within the family" (Croll, 1983: 68).

In summary, gender inequality in the division of domestic labor defines Chinese patriarchy. The confinement of women to the domestic sphere prevents them from competing with men in the public domain and is the root of their subordination. Far from being a trivial matter, division of domestic labor is thus central to the functioning and reproduction of the Chinese patriarchy. The Communist revolution and its many calls for the liberation of women did not eliminate or even reduce this crucial inequality between the sexes. It is in this rather sobering historical context that we discuss how rural-to-urban migration may have transformed entrenched gender inequality in the division of domestic chores and child care. In what follows, we address this question by analyzing the multiple strategies migrant men devise to reconcile their gender role beliefs with socioeconomic realities, and the way they square their notion of manliness with their participation in domestic chores.

GAPS BETWEEN IDEALS AND REALITY

Although they can earn a higher income in the city than in their rural home, work in the city is far from desirable for migrant men. Our respondents included factory workers, cooks, taxi drivers, security guards, hairdressers, and waiters. Their monthly income ranged from eighteen hundred to seven thousand yuan; the median monthly income category was three thousand to 3999 yuan. Although this was a decent amount by rural standards, it was barely enough to maintain a household in the city, given that migrants have to pay private tuition fees if their children live with them , or support two households if their children have been left behind. Furthermore, housing prices and living costs have soared in urban China over the past three decades, but the wages of migrant workers have increased much more slowly. Choi, a forty-four-year-old taxi driver from rural Guangdong, summarized life in the city for migrant workers:

> The exhaustion would not kill you, the hunger would not destroy you, and the wage is never enough.

Many male migrants take two jobs in order to boost their income and thus work extremely long hours (e.g., thirteen to fifteen hours a day) or do physically demanding jobs. Lacking education, skills, capital, useful connections, and a city *hukou,* they are relegated to the lowest stratum of the occupational hierarchy in urban China. The financial contribution of their wives is therefore essential to make ends meet. The majority of the wives in migrant couples and families have paid employment in the city. Most do factory work and take home a monthly income of between two thousand and four thousand yuan. Meng, a twenty-six-year-old cook from Guangxi province, explained:

> Inflation is high, housing is expensive, the wage is low . . . we need to pay rent, pay for our children's education, and give money to my father. How can we have enough? Society changes too fast, things are getting expensive and the wages remain low . . . before she returned to the city to work, we argued about money all the time. . . . Now she works in the city with me and we have some savings. This makes us both happy.

In addition to routine expenditures, most migrant workers are saving to build houses for their sons (likely to cost between two and three hundred thousand yuan) or to pay for their children's education (which costs up to ten thousand yuan per year). This economic reality means that male migrant workers greatly value their wives' participation in any income-generating activity. When migrant men choose a wife, they focus on personality factors such as kindness and being filial, as well as her potential for productive work. A wife must be "willing to work" (*yuangan*) and "able to work" (*nenggan*). Women who refuse to participate in productive work are criticized. Tang, a thirty-one-year-old shoe factory worker from Hunan province, stated,

> A woman cannot just depend on a man, hoping that he will give her clothes and give her food. She needs to work. If she does, her husband will be pleased. . . . If she does not do anything [paid employment], even if her husband is rich, she would be bored.

In spite of the value placed on women's productivity, most migrant men have continued to anchor femininity in women's domestic role and responsibilities. A virtuous woman is one who washes the clothes, tidies up the house, and cooks the meals. A woman who finishes the chores and cooks the meals would score eight out of ten on migrant men's scale of femininity. The centrality of domesticity to their notion of femininity means that many migrant men reject and despise men who assume unconventional family roles. For example, merely mentioning the term "house husband" provoked strong reactions from our respondents. Lau, a thirty-two-year-old grocery store owner from Henan province, stated bluntly,

> I would definitely not let my wife earn money to support me. How could I still be called a man if I do such a thing?

In summary, male migrant workers want their wife to do both paid work and domestic chores, but consider her paid work secondary and her domestic chores the primary aspect of her role as a wife. Secondly, normative ideals of men as providers and men as the "outside" workers notwithstanding, economic necessity often compels men to work both outside and inside the home. Chao, an unemployed male migrant worker from Hunan province, summed up what actually happens:

> Although the norm is such that men are supposed to be in charge [of work] outside and women are responsible for work inside, many couples actually do the work together.

Together perhaps, but certainly not equal, a topic to which we now turn.

MIGRANT MEN AND HOUSEWORK: FOUR PATTERNS

As discussed above, men in rural China do not normally share domestic chores and are not expected to do so. However, many men in migrant couples and families are forced to do more of the domestic chores and child care after migration. Among our respondents, we observed four patterns of response to the challenges of migration in the domestic sphere: extended exemption, strategic avoidance, selective acceptance, and active participation. These patterns of response were related to the husband-wife income ratio, time availability (i.e. working hours and shift arrangements), the family's child care needs, and the migrant man's concept of manliness.

Extended Exemption

Extended exemption describes the response of migrant men who have managed to extend their rural traditional exemption from domestic chores to urban China because their earning power is much higher than that of their migrant wife. This pattern is characterized by the husband doing a minimum number of domestic chores. His status as the primary provider is confirmed. His wife's paid work is considered secondary, and often both husband and wife see her shouldering of most domestic chores as legitimate. Yang, a fifty-two-year-old construction subcontractor from Hubei province, worked with his wife on a construction site. Although his wife was physically stronger than he (and taller), more highly qualified, and had mastered the skills of the trade, she was his assistant on the construction site and did all the chores at home. As he proudly and contentedly told the interviewer: "She shops, cooks, washes, and tidies up."

Yang was never involved in housework back in their village. His ability to extend this traditional division of labor to the couple's migrant life was largely due to his relatively high earning power. As a subcontractor he was earning more than five thousand yuan per month, the highest wage among our male respondents. In the majority of families who had adopted this approach to the division of labor the husband was in his forties or fifties, and there appeared to be a consensus about division of household work; many husbands commented that their wives "refused to let them do any domestic chores." The comments of Fan, a forty-one-year-old taxi driver who was earning four to five thousand yuan per month, were typical:

> She [his wife] is good. She does all the chores at home. Sometimes I want to help, but she does not let me help . . . she wants me to rest after work, to have dinner and sleep. My work is tougher than hers.

Fan was earning a much higher wage than his wife, and he worked longer hours. He considered this important, because he believed that a man's main responsibility is to provide for his family. In contrast, his wife had a job that allowed her to make frequent, regular visits to their rural home to see their children. She assumed responsibility for translocational care, and her lower wage also justified Fan's exemption from domestic chores in the city. Older women's general acceptance that domestic chores are their primary duty—and solely their responsibility—may contribute to migrant men's ability to extend their traditional rural exemption from housework to life in the city after migration. However, we heard of the case of a twenty-three-year-old wife who planned to divorce her twenty-eight-year-old husband because he bossed her around and completely refused to help with any domestic chores. In this particular case the wife had initially been financially dependent on her husband and had little support from her natal family. She had little say in the relationship, and her husband expected her to contribute to the household financially through her full-time work as a beautician, as well as shouldering most of the domestic chores. She complained of exhaustion and was indignant about the unfairness of this arrangement, considering his reluctance to help her with domestic chores symptomatic of his general lack of affection toward her, and she was secretly saving so as to be able to leave the relationship.

Strategic Avoidance

Strategic avoidance is characterized by a vehement resistance to a more equal division of domestic tasks and the devising of strategies to avoid them, regardless of the needs of the family. In the villages women work both outside and inside the home; they cope with this double burden with help from female relatives, e.g. mothers-in-law. In the cities, where migrant couples will usually be on their own, many wives demand that their husbands do domestic chores. Migrant men who do not want to do these chores, and are not in a position to resist their wife's demands (perhaps they earn less than their wife), escape physically or find other ways to avoid housework. Ting's story, given at the beginning of this chapter, is a case in point. Because he was living away from home five days a week, he could not help his wife, who was working as an accounting clerk, to look after their children. His decision had been particularly hard on his wife when their children were young; for example, she complained that when their children were sick at night, she could not reach him for help. Ting admitted that his wife wanted him to move back home, but explained that living at home would make it difficult for him to get to work in the morning. However, he started work at 9:30 a.m. and usually finished at 5:30 p.m., and his commute from home to work took around half an hour; he seldom did overtime and had a relatively regular work schedule. As Ting complained that his wife was "too dominating" and admitted that he always tried to avoid doing housework at home, one may safely conclude that his decision to live in the factory dormitory was a strategy for avoiding housework.

Because he was living in the factory dormitory during the week, Ting had time to watch TV and play snooker with his colleagues after work. He also had time to exercise and go out with his colleagues for a drink in the evening. In the morning, he was able to sleep longer and get up later. If he were living at home, he would have to prepare meals, do the cleaning, and supervise the children's homework every night of the week, because his wife often brought unfinished accounting work home. He would also need to get up early in the morning to help prepare the children's breakfast and take his younger son to school.

Ting thought that men should be responsible for work outside the home, or heavy chores, while women should be in charge of work inside the home. Even when he was at home, he often tried to avoid housework:

> Sometimes I am tired after a whole day's work. . . . I don't want to do anything, but there are lots of things waiting to be done. . . . Sometimes I wait and hope that she will do it, and she waits and hopes that I will do it, and we end up arguing . . . for example, who's going to do the dishes, sweep and mop the floor.

Xu, a thirty-one-year-old taxi driver from rural Guangdong, also tried to avoid housework:

> I guess I am a bit chauvinistic. I think it is women's job to cook, to prepare the vegetables, and to wash clothes. These are women's jobs and they have to do them. . . . My wife asks me to wash the clothes, I refuse. I just ignore her. . . . Or I tell her that I do not know how to wash them properly. I am just lazy, I just want to have fun. My hobby is having fun.

Xu's resistance to housework was related to his beliefs about men and women's responsibilities, but it was also closely related to his gambling addiction. When he was not working, he was gambling. In his own words, "When I gamble, I forget the earth and the sky, and have no sense of time. Sometimes I even forget to eat. Sometimes I do not go home all night or I return home only at dawn." Xu felt guilty that his gambling addiction was affecting the couple's life, and because of this he was reluctant to disregard her request for help with the housework openly; instead, he found excuses to escape and pretended not to hear her requests.

Selective Acceptance

Selective acceptance characterizes migrant men who selectively accept their wives' demands for "help" with some housework and child care, but conceive their role in housework and child care as secondary and flexible. Men who adopted this pattern were happy to "help out" when the chores were physically too demanding for their wife, when she was too busy or too tired, and when they were more skilled at a particular task. Men in this category often made it clear to their wife that they were not in charge of the chores, and that making sure the chores got done was not their responsibility; they had the power and freedom to decide what, when, and how much help they would offer.

When men "help" their wives with domestic chores it does not mean that the couple has transcended the "men outside, women inside" division of labor; in some cases men choose to help out with chores that need to be performed outside the home, e.g., linens that need to be washed in the river, thus symbolically maintaining the boundary between "outside" and "inside" work. Kim, a fifty-three-year-old male migrant from Hunan, explained how he and his wife divided domestic chores:

> When we are at home, she cooks, but if there are guests, I would buy and wash the vegetables, set the table. We do it together . . . because her back often hurts, so she washes small clothing items and I wash the big items such as linens. She washes at home and I wash outside.

Even though Kim claimed that he and his wife "do it together," he also stressed the distinctions between big and small, and outside and inside; these distinctions are dichotomies male migrant workers mobilize to demarcate the boundaries between the male and female realms, and to highlight the differences between men and women.

In other cases, migrant men chose the tasks they liked, cared about, or considered it gender-appropriate to help with; for example many did not mind playing with their children. Lau, a thirty-two-year-old grocery store owner, prepared meals for the family because he disliked his wife's cooking. Ho, a twenty-five-year-old taxi driver, would help his wife with the mopping of dirty floors and changing the duvet covers, but he absolutely refused to wash the clothes or do the dishes, because he regarded these as feminine tasks. Perhaps it is because the image of rural Chinese women washing clothes in the river has become such a strong symbol of femininity that many male migrant workers refuse to wash clothes. Mopping and sweeping floors and cleaning the toilet are also high on the list of unmanly chores, because they have low status. Washing dishes is considered a womanly chore by some men, because it requires no physical strength and no skill. On the other hand many men consider meal preparation gender-neutral. In the village, men sometimes help to cook for wedding banquets, religious ceremonies, and festival gatherings. In the city, most of the cooks are male. Shopping is considered gender-neutral because it is performed outside the home, in public areas. Choosing the tasks they agree to do—selective acceptance—not only means that male migrants can avoid chores considered unpleasant and unmanly, it also gives them flexibility—they can do domestic tasks when it suits them or when they are "in the mood." Many of the chores that men choose have a leisure component.

Active Participation

The active participants in housework endure peer pressure because of their unconventional role in the domestic realm, and because they are often forced to accept low-status jobs to enable them to combine work with domestic responsibilities. Thirty-six of the eighty-one migrant men in couple and family migration in our sample were doing half or more than half of the household chores. Yau, a thirty-one-year-old factory worker, and Lam, a twenty-year-old waiter from Sichuan province, proudly claimed that they did most of the chores at home without their partners pushing them, including washing and mopping the floor, and washing and folding the laundry. As Lam said,

> She does not need to do housework, I do most of it. Since we moved in together, she has not washed the clothes more than five times, I have been the one who washed our clothes. . . . However, after I sweep the floor, she always sweeps it again because she thinks that I do not clean it properly. We prepare meals together. She stir-fries and I wash and cut the vegetables. Washing the dishes is definitely my job. And we shop for food together.

Other actively participating men, however, were much more reserved about their unconventional role in the household, and often tried to downplay their share of domestic chores to maintain an image of gender respectability. For instance Lin, a forty-seven-year-old subcontractor from Hunan province, said at first that his wife did all the domestic work, but later explained that he "helped" to cook when she was working overtime. As a factory worker she worked overtime almost five days a week, meaning that in practice he cooked for them at least five days a week. Lin not only downplayed his share of domestic chores, he also insisted that the traditional pattern of "men outside, women inside" was maintained when his wife was at home. He trivialized his increased domestic role by claiming that there was little work to be done at home and rationalized the sharing of meal preparation, for example, by citing health and hygiene concerns:

> When my wife is here, of course she does the housework. Now she has returned to our village, I do it. There is little to be done anyway. I cook, wash the few clothes that I have. . . . (Interviewer: And if she works overtime, who cooks then?) Oh right, Me. I cook. . . . You see, we have a family, right? It is impossible that we eat out all the time. I am also concerned about the food hygiene in the shops.

Lin's work as a construction subcontractor was physically very demanding (cu huo), but involved much shorter working hours than his wife's factory work. He was working nine hours a day starting at 8:00 a.m. and finishing around 5:00 p.m. His wife, on the other hand, often had to work overtime until 11:00 p.m. Given Lin's much shorter working hours, it was not surprising that he was doing more chores than his wife. Many migrant construction workers living with factory-worker wives have admitted to doing many of the domestic chores.

However, rather than being proud of his contribution to the household work, Lin felt obliged to justify his role, and saw his involvement in domestic work as a compromise forced on him by his family's circumstances, commenting that "Even if you are not used to it [doing housework], you need to get used to it." It may be that Lin downplayed his share in the domestic chores because he firmly believed that a man's main duty to his family was that of provider. Huang, a thirty-six-year-old taxi driver also did more housework than his wife on weekdays. Although he did not downplay his participation, he still opined that "women are better than men at housework." This linking of housework to the "essential nature" and "natural abilities" of women was quite common among our respondents and their spouses, with quite a few men reporting that their wife would redo the chores that they had done, because their performance did not meet her standards.

Other migrant men who were doing at least half the domestic chores were in dual-earner households and had school-age children. They took a pragmatic approach to the division of domestic chores, suggesting that the division was mostly based on time availability. Liang, a thirty-six-year-old skilled worker from Henan, put it matter-of-factly:

> There is no "division of labor." The person who has time does it. You cannot say that men don't do housework, and that women have to do it all. We men cannot support women financially. If she [one's wife] does not need to work, of course she should do it. But if she is working full time like you, you cannot ask her to do all of it. Because I have more time than her [his wife], I usually do more.

On weekdays Liang does more housework than his wife; on their days off, she does more, and she does not let him do it. Lo was a forty-year-old factory worker from Guangxi province. His seven-year-old son was living with him and his wife in the city, so the couple—who worked in the same factory—took different shifts to enable them to combine work and child care. "We specifically asked to work different shifts. If she works the day shift, I do the night shift. We are in the same team and we swap our shifts every half month." When his wife was doing the night shift, he delivered their son to school and did the shopping before going to work; after work he would also make his son dinner and supervise his homework. For Lo this was the only solution available, because his salary of four thousand yuan was not enough to support the family; having two salaries had also enabled them to bring their son to study in the city.

Du was a thirty-four-year-old engineer, and his wife of five years owned a lingerie shop in Dongguan. The couple were both Sichuan natives, and they met in Dongguan in 2003. During the daytime his wife's shop was not busy, so she cooked and looked after their three-year-old child. In the evenings, when she was busy with customers, Du took over child care duties. He also cooked and took care of their child on his days off and during weekends, because his wife was usually very busy with customers at these times. For Du this was an arrangement that accommodated their respective work schedules. Liang, Lo, and Du were all in relationships with a fairly equal division of labor and marital power between the sexes. This makes one wonder whether an equal division of domestic work depends on more than time availability and child care requirements, being more a reflection of the status of the woman in the relationship and her bargaining power.

Men who do more housework than their wives sometimes feel the peer pressure. Yao (a forty-five-year-old security guard), whose story we mentioned in chapter 1, told us,

> I wash her clothes, I cook, and I clean. But when I hang up the wet laundry in the balcony, I worry that our neighbors see me doing it. I am afraid other people will see it. It does not look good. . . . I would never tell people that I wash my wife's clothes. . . . I would never tell other people. When people ask, I tell them that I don't do chores, to save face.

Yao was particularly concerned that his fellow Henanese would find out that he washes his wife's underwear. In fact, he had already been teased about this. He did not have many friends and was not keen on meeting coethnics, because he was sure that they would tease him about his unconventional role in the family:

> I don't want my friends to know that I am washing the clothes. When they ask, I deny it. Other Henanese would tease me—Ha ha, you even wash your wife's underwear!—I say, "Of course I don't wash her underwear."

Zhang is a thirty-four-year-old security guard from Henan province who took a low-status job as a security guard so that he could return frequently to his rural home to visit his elderly parents and two left-behind children (see chapter 2). It was very difficult for Zhang's wife to get leave from her factory job. On the other hand, Zhang's boss would give him up to four months leave per year, spread over two periods. Zhang's decision to take up the low-paid (around two thousand and five hundred yuan per month) and low-status security job thus allowed him to combine paid employment with translocal care responsibility. However, this had been a difficult choice, because Zhang despised his job as a security guard, commenting,

> It is a job without any prospects. . . . It has no status. We are like a dog watching the door. . . . You do not even need to use your physical strength [in the job of security guard]. You learn no skills. . . . What you do all day is register the cars that come in.

While some active participants, such as Yau and Lam, may not be embarrassed by their participation in housework, this was not the case for many of the men who did an equal or majority share of the housework, such as Lin and Liang. It is even more problematic for men who face peer pressure as a result of their unconventional role in the household (Yao), or who have to accept low-status jobs in order to combine work and family responsibilities, such as Zhang. Rather than being seen as pioneers of gender equality, the men who work as equal partners in the domestic domain are often ridiculed by their neighbors and peers as "wife slaves" (*laoponu*). In order to reconcile the contradiction between Chinese patriarchal ideology—which judges manliness on the basis of a man's public role—and their active participation in domestic chores, men who take an equal share in domestic work have legitimized their new role using a discourse of masculinity that anchors manhood on loyalty and dedication to, and care of, their family.

HOUSEWORK AND MASCULINITY

As suggested, some migrant men have participated actively in housework despite social and peer pressure. Some of this group attempt to downplay their role, some have to fend off the mockery of their peers, and some have to sacrifice their self-esteem, accepting a low-status job that allows them to combine their work and family responsibilities. It is men in this last group, who share in the domestic work but find doing so problematic, who are most likely to legitimize their unconventional domestic role through a discourse of manhood that is based on men's care for and loyalty to their families, and their responsibility to maintain family happiness and marital harmony. It contrasts hard-working migrant men—who sacrifice personal pride for their family's well-being—with urban entrepreneurs who are corrupted by their new wealth and let their uncontrolled sexuality ruin their family.

As rural migrants to the city, all of these respondents were acutely aware of two hegemonic ideals of city manhood: monied manhood and quality manhood. Monied manhood is epitomized by the rich, success-ful, and well-connected entrepreneur. Quality manhood is exemplified by the highly educated, skilled, well-mannered professional. Wealth—in the form of cars, houses, and mistresses—is the measure of monied manhood, whereas quality manhood is judged in terms of knowledge and professional skills. Although some of our respondents hoped to achieve hegemonic ideal manhood, perhaps through setting up their own business, acquiring skills, or supporting their sons through univer-sity, many were also aware of the formidable obstacles in their way. More than one third of our respondents had set up a business that had eventually failed, costing them their savings. Some were still hopeful that they would eventually become a boss, but many were resigned to the fact that without capital, education, skills, experience, and connec-tions they would forever be trapped in a life of *dagong* in cities. *Dagong* means earning a wage so meager that the worker can barely meet his or her city living expenses and support family in the village; it is a life with-out prospects or hope. For most of our respondents, a *dagong* man is the equivalent of a coolie; *dagong* life is bitter, lonely, exhausting, and monotonous. *Dagong* encompasses the separation from their family and discrimination from the locals that migrant workers have to endure; migrant workers are outsiders in the city and have to put up with being treated rudely, especially in the case of service workers. Many migrant men said that they went out to *dagong* so that their children would be able to escape the *dagong* life of a migrant worker. It was this sense of self-sacrifice, and their hopes for their children, that had given many of our respondents a sense of meaning; they were disillusioned with *dagong* life in the city and psychologically crushed by the chasm between the reality of this life and the hegemonic ideals of monied and quality man-hood. They constructed what we have termed the concept of "respect-able manhood"—a sense of masculinity based on the effort a man makes to fulfill his responsibility to provide and care for his family and make them happy.

Respectable manhood prioritizes morality over material wealth and values pragmatic adaptation above unrealistic aspirations. The concept of respectable manhood posits that a man's success is measured not in terms of material outcomes but according to the efforts he makes to provide for his family in the broader sense, i.e. making provision for his children's future and ensuring their emotional well-being. It stresses the importance of working honestly, i.e. doing the right thing and earning clean money. A manual laborer who earns a meager wage by "working hard with his two hands" is regarded as more honorable than a parasitic, unproductive, second-generation rich person (*fu er dai*) or a second-generation official (*guan er dai*) who inherited wealth from his parents and has only known a life of conspicuous consumption.

A man who adheres to the notion of respectable manhood resists the colonization of private life by money, and views money as being too often a source of evil and family ruin. The ideology of respectable manhood lauds migrant men for their family harmony and marital stability and deprecates rich city entrepreneurs for being corrupted by money, as well as for marital infidelity that is likely to lead to divorce. This construction of respectable manhood distinguishes between rural pragmatism and urban aspiration, and extols peasant migrant workers' ability to swallow the bitterness of *dagong* life, to accept low-status work, and adapt to living conditions in the city. According to the discourse of respectable manhood, family life and family harmony are the ultimate measure of a man's success, and educated men's reluctance to get married and assume responsibility for a family is perplexing.

Interestingly, it is this family-oriented concept of respectable manhood that most of the men who participated actively in domestic chores and child care have used to legitimize their unconventional domestic role and maintain a sense of dignity and meaning in their life. Lo, the forty-year-old factory worker who was doing shift work so that both he and his wife could work and also care for their seven-year-old son, rejected a definition of manhood based on economic success. He treasured being with his wife and son in the city and saw his participation in domestic chores as a pragmatic choice, which enabled the family to remain together. Yao, the forty-five-year-old security guard who cooked and washed his wife's clothes, rationalized his unconventional role by reference to his love for his wife and the children; he valued family happiness and harmony highly. He was earning less than his wife and reconciled this status conflict by defining manhood in terms of putting family before career. Zhang, the thirty-four-year-old man who had taken a low-status job as a security guard in the city so that he could combine work with translocal care of his left-behind children and elderly parents, rationalized the sacrifice he had made in order to fulfill his caregiving responsibilities by stressing that "we village people are pragmatic . . . we work hard to earn our living . . . my only principle is to make my family happy." He also rejected the hegemonic ideal of monied manhood, claiming that "money is not everything; rich people are not necessarily happy. We rural migrants are not less happy than other people."

Likewise, he was ambivalent about the values of quality manhood, the idea that manliness resides in professionalism, education, and skill. He compared himself with his wife's brother, a university graduate who has been unemployed for years because "he does not want to earn small money and lacks the ability to earn big money." Zhang was critical of his brother-in-law's unrealistic aspirations and perplexed by his reluctance to get married. He summed up this cultural disparity by saying that "we village people are different from city folks. For us, no wife means no life. If you are over thirty and still single, village people will think that you are abnormal." Although the concept of respectable manhood is constructed by male migrant workers as a form of resistance to the two hegemonic ideals of monied and quality manhood that sustain their cultural marginalization in the city, it also serves as a discourse for the legitimization of the unconventional domestic role that *dagong* life imposes on men who are part of a migrant couple and/or family.

CONCLUSION

The novel context provided by rural-to-urban migration makes negotiation of housework an important issue for couples. As our analysis has shown, migrant men respond differently to the change in circumstances. Migrant men's response to the housework question follows one of four patterns: extended exemption, strategic avoidance, selective acceptance, or active participation. Some resourceful, older men are able to extend their traditional rural exemption from housework to life in the city after migration. Some younger migrant men capitalize on their wife's low status in the relationship to make sure that the traditional division of labor is preserved in the city. Other men strategically avoid housework, and some regard themselves as "helpers," selectively accepting the tasks that they enjoy, care about, or consider gender-appropriate. Some migrant men actively participate in domestic chores and child care, taking on an equal or majority share of the work. Some in this group attempt to downplay their role, some have to withstand the ridicule of their peers, and some have to sacrifice their pride, accepting a low-status job that allows them to combine work and family responsibilities.

The factors that influence migrant men's attitude to housework include the husband-to-wife income ratio, the partners' respective availability, the age of children, and the migrant man's concept of manhood. This is particularly relevant to migrant men who participate actively in housework and child care; this group has developed a discourse of masculinity that stresses men's dedication to and care of the family, and their responsibility for maintaining family happiness and marital harmony. This family-oriented discourse of masculinity contrasts hard-working migrant men who sacrifice personal pride for their family's well-being with urban entrepreneurs who are corrupted by their new wealth and let their uncontrolled sexuality ruin their family. It is therefore a counterdiscourse of manhood that rehabilitates migrant men after the humiliation they have experienced as second-class citizens and marginalized workers in the cities, and the disjunction this represents with their dominant position in rural China. This counterdiscourse underlies inequality between migrant men and women, and between urban and rural men, and simultaneously serves as an engine for changing the unequal gender stratification based on the "outside, inside" divide.

CHAPTER 6

Migration, Fatherhood, and Emotionality

Shen was a line operator in an electronics factory operated by a Taiwanese enterprise when we interviewed him in Shenzhen in early 2013. Born in 1977, he was in his mid-thirties and is the father of two young daughters. Shen is from a rural village in Henan province, a large source of migrant workers in central China. He left his hometown and migrated to Dongguan for the first time in October 2000, after his first daughter was born and the family's expenses increased dramatically. Seven years later his second daughter was born, and he felt greater financial pressure. Working eleven hours a day in the labor-intensive factory, Shen earned three thousand yuan per month and sent two thousand to twenty-five hundred yuan back home to support the daughters he had left behind. Shen's migration and working experiences are not much different from the stories of millions of male migrant workers who migrate to cities to make a living. What makes his case impressive is his profound love for his daughters, demonstrated in his narrative, and the anguish and guilt he felt because of his long-term separation from them. Shen left his first daughter with his wife and parents when she was a toddler. Soon after, Shen's wife also migrated for work in the city. The couple did not return to their native village until their second daughter was three years old. In the previous twelve years, Shen had spent very limited time with his elder daughter. Just like many line operators in labor-intensive factories in the Pearl River Delta, Shen found it hard to ask for leave to visit his family in Henan province. The Spring Festival was his only opportunity to have some quality time with his daughters. Although Shen sent the majority of his income to support his family, and bought whatever his daughters asked for to compensate for his long-term physical absence in their lives, he admitted that his elder daughter was emotionally distant from him. Even if she called Shen "Dad" and said "thank you" for the clothes he bought for her, he felt that his elder daughter, deep in her heart, was keeping an emotional distance from him, and their communication was rare and not close.

Shen recalled a sad story about his elder daughter in his interview. On her third birthday, her grandparents bought the girl a birthday cake to celebrate. However, she insisted on waiting for her parents before she blew out the candles. At that time, Shen worked in Dongguan and his wife worked in Shenzhen. Neither of them could go back for her birthday. The poor girl waited for her parents until eleven o'clock at night and eventually fell asleep sitting at the table with the cake in front of her. Shen heard this story when he made a call to his parents the next day. He could not help crying on the phone. Shen felt so guilty that the next year he asked for leave from his factory in advance and returned to his rural home to celebrate his daughter's birthday. What he did not anticipate during his visit was another heartbreaking episode. When he arrived at the village, his elder daughter ran to him, held his hand with one hand and embraced his thigh with her other arm, and announced to her little friends: "See, I told you I have a dad." Because Shen left home for work in the cities when his elder daughter was only three months old and did not return for two years, the children in his neighborhood had been teasing his daughter that she was a poor girl without a father. Shen's daughter felt aggrieved and was unable to hold back from telling her friends that she did have a father. These heart-rending experiences not only made Shen feel guilty about his daughters, but also made him realize that his remittances could never make up for his physical absence in their lives. As he told us in the interview, "What the children want is not necessarily the money. What they want is that we (as parents) can be there to say 'Happy Birthday' to them on their birthdays."

Compared to his relationship with his elder daughter, Shen's relationship with his younger daughter was good; as he said, "My second daughter is emotionally close to me." This is mainly because his second daughter had lived with Shen and his wife in Shenzhen and had been raised by them until she was three years old. After the poignant scenes with his elder daughter and the reflecting he had done since their occurrence, Shen wanted to raise his younger daughter with his wife in

Shenzhen. However, Shen's wife disagreed with him on this matter. She believed that the tuition fee (five thousand yuan per year) of the kindergarten their younger daughter attended was too high and decided to send her back to their native village, where the tuition was much lower. Given the incomes of Shen and his wife, it was hard to argue that his wife's considerations were not reasonable. Even so, Shen fought with his wife for two days on this matter. He accused his wife of being niggardly to their young daughter and argued that the education service in the cities was much better than that in their village. His wife accused Shen of wasting money and spoiling their younger daughter by buying whatever she asked for. Shen argued that whatever he bought for his daughters was in his affordable range, but his wife argued that, for their two daughters' future, they should save as much as possible. Shen admitted that, in his fights with his wife, he was always the one who lost. This time was no exception. He finally conceded and let his wife take their younger daughter back to their native village. Leaving his younger daughter behind is very painful for Shen. As he recalled, once he phoned his younger daughter, and the girl told him: "Dad, I miss you so much. I miss you so much that I cry. When will you come back to visit me?" All Shen could promise is that he would visit her at the coming Spring Festival. But he knew that a short visit during the Spring Festival would not be enough for either of them.

Although Shen comes from a village in North China where the patrilineal ideology favors sons instead of daughters, he said that he and his parents love his two daughters very much and that he did not plan to have a son. The increased financial pressure of raising another child is the main reason for that decision. In Shen's life, the happiest thing is that he has two adorable daughters. He said, "No matter how hard and how laborious my work in the cities is, I feel it worthy. Whenever I hear my two little girls call me Daddy, I feel all my hard work is worthwhile."

EMOTIONALITY IN MASCULINITY AND FATHERHOOD

Shen's case reveals an understudied issue in the existing literature of masculinity and fatherhood in Chinese societies: emotionality. In both Western and Eastern societies, men are usually defined or described as rational, instrumental, and independent. Being emotional and expressing emotion are always associated with femininity and defined as female characteristics. As stated in Connell's analysis of masculinity (1998), in many patriarchal societies, what men do is usually what women do not do and vice versa. When being emotional is characterized as feminine, it is excluded from the realm of manhood. Thus, in many patriarchal societies, being an emotional man means being a weak man and has negative connotations that may even threaten a man's gender identity. However, the culturally normative decoupling of masculinity and emotion does not mean that men do not have any feelings. Social suppression of male emotionality and the cultural emphasis of rationality in conventional masculinity do not necessarily lead men to become unemotional. Some studies (Fernández et al., 2000; Montes, 2013) have pointed out that the types of emotions men and women can express are determined by the culture and gendered ideology of a particular society. In other words, emotions are gendered and embedded in sociocultural contexts. Whereas emotions such as sadness, worry, and anguish are directly linked to femininity in many societies, some assertive emotions, "such as anger, pride, and independence," are associated with masculinity (Fernández et al., 2000; Montes, 2013: 471). Moreover, the "new man" image that emerged in Western societies in the 1980s is regarded as the starting point from which the expression of emotions and emotionality was no longer defined as mutually exclusive vis à vis rationality; it became an acceptable way of defining contemporary masculinity and, in many cases, fatherhood (Dermott, 2008). The "new dad" image that emerged in the West in the 1990s further promoted both public and academic openness toward men's emotional expression and attracted more academic attention to men's emotionality (Dermott, 2008).

In the twentieth century, the essence of fatherhood in Western societies was economically providing for one's children (Atkinson and Blackwelder, 1993). Since the late twentieth century, "the social definitions of the fathering role have changed from that of provider to nurturer" (Atkinson and Blackwelder, 1993: 976). The "new dad" discourse shifted the conventional focus on men's public lives and their breadwinning capacity in constructing their fatherhood as well as their masculinity toward a new attention on men's personal relationships, such as the "quality and negotiation of the father-child relationship," and the role of men's emotions in these relationships (Dermott, 2008: 65). Compared to the traditional image of the father who is an emotionally distant and inaccessible provider, the "new dad" has more involvement in his children's daily care, has close contact with his children, and develops more of an emotional attachment to his children (Brandth and

Kvande, 1998; Dermott, 2008). In the "new dad" discourse, "care and intimacy with children" is a new territory that men in contemporary societies need to conquer (Brandth and Kvande, 1998: 309). A man's capacity in mastering a new challenge in child care is thus regarded as "an important masculine attribute" (Brandth and Kvande, 1998: 309). In this sense, the intimate and emotional element in the "new dad" image does not threaten men's masculinity construction in contemporary Western societies. On the contrary, it becomes a new platform for men to demonstrate their masculine characteristics.

On the other hand, mass international migration caused by the economic inequality between areas creates a new context for understanding masculinity and fatherhood in both Western and Eastern societies. It has offered new opportunities for migrant men, especially those from developing societies, to reflect on their masculinity and fatherhood. Existing studies (Osella and Osella, 2000; Walter et al., 2004; Broughton, 2008; Parreñas, 2008) on the intersection of migration, masculinity, and fatherhood mainly focused on economic dimensions and argued that the increased breadwinning capacity brought by international migration enables migrant men from developing societies to display their manhood by remittances, gifts, and generous consumption. Being a successful patriarchal provider is central to migrant men's masculinity, maintaining their positions as the heads of their households even if they are not physically present in their houses and fulfilling their duties as responsible fathers (Osella and Osella, 2000; Walter et al., 2004; Broughton, 2008).

Despite the overwhelming focus of previous studies on the economic dimensions of migrant labor, some nascent studies (e.g., Montes, 2013) have analyzed the emotional dimension of masculinity and fatherhood in migrant men. For example, in her study of Guatemalan migrant men, Montes (2013: 469) argued that international migration and long-term physical separation from their families in their home country offered a new opportunity for migrant men to "reflect on their emotional relations" with their distant family members, especially their children. She also indicated that international migration provided a channel for migrant men to vent their emotions, which were usually suppressed. Among the emotions experienced by migrant men in the process of migrating from Guatemala to the United States, some emotions, such as love and concern, arose from their intimate relationships with their family members, whereas some emotions, such as anguish, devastation, worry, and sacrifice, were caused by their international migration per se. Montes (2013) concluded that Guatemalan migrant men's emotional expressions and reflection on their emotions are challenges to or resistance toward the hegemonic masculinity that defines men as unemotional and nonnurturing.

Compared to the rich literature on international migration and its effects on masculinity and fatherhood in Western and other Asian societies, discussion of the intersection of migration and masculinity/fatherhood in Chinese societies is rare. In Chinese societies, gendered parenthood ideology and parenting practices are greatly affected by Chinese cultural values, particularly Confucianism, which emphasizes the importance of family, the responsibilities of parents, and the parental duty to raise well-adjusted children (Wu et al., 2002). Traditionally, the father is the economic supporter, moral instructor, and stern disciplinarian of his children (Jankowaik, 2011). The father-child relationship in Chinese society is shaped by the ideology of filial piety, which encourages children's "total obedience, respect and loyalty toward the father" (Jankowiak, 2011: 110). Due to the filial obligation, an authoritarian approach is observed in Chinese fathering and is mainly expressed by the father's close surveillance of his children, especially in their early years (Holroyd, 2003; Ward, 1989). To construct and maintain an authoritarian image of the father, traditional Chinese fathers are emotionally detached from their children. In childrearing, the emotional work is usually associated with motherhood or maternal practices. In postsocialist China, although gendered parenthood is still stable, some changes in parenting practices have been observed because of economic developments, social transformations, and changed social norms and values. In cities, due to factors including the one-child policy, parents' exposure to Western culture and parenting ideologies, and the mothers' increased education level, authoritarian parenting is gradually fading, and a flexible and reasoned control of children is gradually being adopted by Chinese parents (Xu et al., 2005). With women's increased participation in the labor force and the influence of gender equality, fathers in urban China are observed to have more participation in the physical and emotional care of children and to pay more attention to their emotional connections with their children (Jankowiak, 2011). Compared to parents in cities, rural parents have kept to traditional parenting, which emphasizes the children's obedience to the parents and women's role in childrearing (Ho, 1989). However, with millions of rural men migrating to cities and becoming internal migrant fathers, traditional fathering practices in rural China are facing the challenges and influences of various factors, ranging from economic to cultural. In this context, how does internal migration reshape fatherhood and father-child relations among rural-to-urban migrants in postsocialist China? How do these migrant men reflect on their fatherhood in and through their migration process? What kinds of emotions do they vent or experience in their migration process? How do they understand and interpret the emotions they experienced as migrant fathers? These are the questions explored in this chapter.

MIGRANT FATHERS AND THEIR LEFT-BEHIND CHILDREN

Structural Obstacles, Economic Constraints, and Paternal Emotions

Although mass internal migration has existed in China for more than three decades, the stringent rural-urban divide and the household-registration system force many migrant parents to leave their children behind in their rural home. Even though some urban areas have been loosening their control over migrant workers, and the central government has been gradually relaxing its household-registration control in recent years, there were still more than twenty-two million school-age left-behind children in China in 2011 (The Ministry of Education of the People's Republic of China, 2011). Among our 192 male respondents, 76 have left-behind children aged fifteen or under. Most of these left-behind children are being raised by their wives and parents or parents-in-law. Under the current household-registration system, the children of migrant workers, who do not have an urban *hukou*, still have only limited access to child care services, education services, and medical insurance in cities. This limited access creates structural obstacles for migrant workers to bring their children to cities. In addition to these structural obstacles, the discrepancy between the low incomes of most migrant workers and the high cost of living in cities is another important factor that forces them to leave their children behind in rural China. Although the continuous labor shortage in the past decade forced employers to increase wages for migrant workers (Choi and Peng, 2015), their income was still slim compared to the consumption level in cities. According to data provided by China's National Bureau of Statistics, the average salary of migrant workers increased from 495 yuan in 1995 to 1,690 yuan in 2010 (Lu, 2012). In 2010, the average income of urban citizens in Shenzhen was 4,205 yuan per month and the average consumption was nineteen hundred yuan per month.[1] Zhao, a forty-seven-year-old taxi driver in Shenzhen, who is a father of one adult son and two school-age daughters, compared his income and expenses in Shenzhen:

> It is hard for me to afford two school-age daughters. Let me calculate my income and the expenses for you. My monthly income is a little bit over four thousand yuan. I spend two thousand yuan on renting a small apartment in Shenzhen. All the bills cost me about one hundred yuan per month. My daily food consumption and cigarette consumption is about fifty yuan. I give each daughter eight hundred yuan per month as their allowance. I have no savings by the end of the month. In 2008, I earned five to six thousand yuan per month and the expenses were less than three thousand yuan per month. That time was much better than nowadays. Now, my monthly income ranges from three to four thousand yuan. All expenses in Shenzhen increased, doubled, but my income decreased. What can I do? I have no savings in these years. As working-class people, it is impossible for us to think about settling down in a city like Shenzhen.

As Zhao can barely support himself in Shenzhen, he had to leave his two school-aged daughters with his elderly parents. As a divorced man in his mid-forties, Zhao admitted that he wanted to live with his daughters. However, the harsh reality forced him to live alone in Shenzhen. As he indicated,

> Who would be willing to live alone? Nobody. Everybody wants to live with his/her family. . . . Of course, I dreamed of living with my daughters in Shenzhen. Sending them to schools in Shenzhen? Is it possible? I know it is better for them to come to Shenzhen and study in Shenzhen. [If they were in Shenzhen] we could see each other every day. We could take care of each other. However, I cannot afford their expenses in Shenzhen. With my slim income, I dare not to think about that [bringing his daughters to Shenzhen]. I have no choice but leaving them behind in the village. At least, they can go to school there.

Economic pressure is not only the justification used by migrant parents to defend their long-term separation from their children, but also the reason they use to persuade their left-behind children to accept the painful reality: a long-term separation from their migrant parents. Yu, a fifty-two-year-old construction worker from Hunan province and the father of four adult children, used the metaphor of parent swallows raising their babies to explain the separation to their children. As he stated,

> We [Yu and his wife] left them [their children] when they were very young. . . . We visited them once a year, in the Spring Festival, for several days. . . . My

---

1. http://finance.jrj.com.cn/2011/04/25111898813726.shtml

wife once pointed at the nest of swallows under the roof of our house and explained it to my children: "Look at the swallows. We, the parents, are just like the swallows. The swallows fly out to get the food and fly back to feed their babies. Our migration to cities is just like that. We went to the cities to earn money. Without the swallow parents flying out to get the food, the baby swallows would have nothing to eat. If your dad and I had not worked in the cities, you would not have food, or clothes, and you would not have money to pay for your tuition fee.

Breadwinning capacity is a key element in defining fatherhood and masculinity in both Western and Eastern societies (Dermott, 2008; Brandth and Kvande, 1998). The ability to economically provide for their children and families is a major basis on which these male migrant workers construct their manhood and fatherhood. Although many migrant fathers in our study argued that the increased breadwinning capacity brought by migration and the remittances they sent back were crucial to their stay-behind family members' well-being, the economic support, which is the typical way of being a responsible father, cannot prevent the pain and emotional costs experienced by both migrant fathers and their left-behind children due to long-term physical separation. In contrast to the stereotype of unemotional, rational fathers, many migrant fathers in our study demonstrated very strong emotions in their narratives regarding their separation from their children. Most of them reported how strongly they missed their left-behind children and found it natural to express this kind of emotion. They did not associate strongly missing their children with being vulnerable and weak, but interpreted it as a natural love expressed by them as fathers. As Ou, a thirty-four-year-old security guard from Henan and a migrant father of two children, said,

> As a man, I missed my son much more than my wife did. I always miss my son. One night, I dreamed of him. My wife told me: "I heard you talk in your sleep last night. You mumbled the name of our son in your sleep." I think that is because I missed him so much. Frankly speaking, I think it is quite normal to miss your children.

In addition to missing their children, many migrant fathers recalled the pain, guilt, anguish, and worry they experienced when they were separated from their children. As Kwan, a forty-one-year-old father of two sons, stated,

> I left my son for work in the cities when he was one year old. I did not spend much quality time with him. . . . If I had the opportunity to start it again, I would choose to stay at home. When he was very young, like two or three years old, he was very adorable. Every time I visited him in my native village,

I was reluctant to leave. When I had to leave, when I was in the railway station, I dared not to look back. Because, when I had to leave, he would chase me and cry. He cried so hard that it made me extremely sad, but I could not take him with me.

Lee, a thirty-year-old electrician from rural Guangdong, worried that his daughter would not even recognize him when he returned home:

Sometimes, when I think about my daughter, I feel much sorrow. I miss her so much. . . . I left her when she was one year old. I do not have much time to stay at home and keep her company. I don't have much contact with her. Sometimes, I worry that she may not recognize me when I return.

Bai, a forty-two-year-old worker from Guangxi, blamed himself for not being able to be there for his children:

I miss my wife and children very much. . . . I don't think I am a very good father. When they [his children] were young, I was not there with them. As a father, how to say it, I think my concern and care for them is not enough.

Although some fathers' guilt and sorrow derive from their physical absence in their children's daily lives, other fathers' guilt and anguish come from their inability to provide their children with good economic support and other benefits when compared to what urban men can provide for their children. As Ai, a forty-year-old taxi driver from rural Guangdong and a father of three children, stated,

I feel I have failed my children. I cannot earn enough money to purchase an apartment for them in the city. I cannot provide them with a higher allowance. I don't know how to tutor them to do their homework. I don't know how to express my feelings. I feel I have failed my children. They are very smart. They are good at their study. If I had provided them with more [resources and benefits], what would they look like now? I can't fall asleep when I think about things like this at night.

Similarly, Chiu, a fifty-three-year-old construction worker from rural Guangdong and a migrant father of three children, blamed himself for not being able to support his elder daughter's education:

I have three children. The eldest one is a daughter and the younger ones are two sons. I migrated when they were young. I didn't help them with their study. My daughter didn't finish her study in junior high school. At that time, it was impossible for me to afford three children's tuition fees. . . . She dropped out of school when she was fourteen, fifteen years old. She migrated to cities for work. I felt sorry for her. I felt heartbroken. She was a little girl and she had to migrate for work. I had no choice.

Some fathers felt depressed and heartbroken when their children displayed recalcitrant behavior in front of them and were emotionally distant from them. These fathers felt that they had lost their authority as fathers in front of their children because of their longtime absence in their children's lives and blamed themselves for not being able to earn more money or be successful (*you benshi*). Fei, a forty-three-year-old construction worker from Henan and a father of two children, told us his dilemma of being a migrant father: while he has been able to support his children through migrant work, he has failed to develop emotional bonds with them:

> My relationship with my son is not good. Even if I made money [by working in the cities], I lost my son's love. He doesn't listen to me, but to his mom. . . . For example, he was skating, I went there and asked him to come back home for dinner. He ignored me. . . . I felt heartbroken. . . . I have to make money. But, he doesn't understand that. He thinks it is me who makes myself a migrant worker. No way out. I have no choice. I am not blaming him. I blame myself because I am not economically successful. If I owned a factory in the city and had a lot of money, I would bring him to the city and accompany him all days. That would be different.

In addition to economic support, some migrant fathers also compared their fathering practices with those of local urban men and felt guilty when they saw local urban fathers having a good time playing with their children whereas they, as migrant fathers, could scarcely spend any time with their children most of the year. As Li, a twenty-five-year-old taxi driver whom we met in Dongguan, a father of two young children, said,

> I am not a good father. As a father, I am not like those local rich men. Those local men can play with their children, such as taking them to the shopping mall at weekends. They have more time to play with their children. But, we, as migrant workers, seldom have time to play with our children. What we can do is economically supporting them. Except for that, there is nothing we can do for them because we can visit them only once a year, for several days.

Emotional Turmoil and Coping Strategies

As Montes (2013: 481) pointed out, migration creates the opportunity for migrant fathers to "get in touch with deeper emotions that would be overlooked under normal circumstances as a result of the social association with feminine identities." Instead of feeling emotional expressions as a threat to their masculinity, many migrant fathers in our study felt it natural to vent their various emotions about their children in the interviews, such as their profound love and concern for their children and the guilt, sorrow, and regret they felt for missing their children's growth. These emotional expressions, to some extent, indicated that migrant fathers experienced similar emotional turmoil as migrant mothers in their migration and separation from their children (Hondagneu-Sotelo and Avila, 1997; Parreñas, 2001). By being physically separated from their children for a long time, migrant fathers realized how deep their love and concern for their children was, even if they seldom openly expressed those emotions in normal circumstances. By comparing their fathering experiences with those of local men, the migrant fathers realized what they had missed in the migration process, and its emotional cost. Migration also exposed these migrant fathers to urban parenting practices, especially the things urban fathers can provide for and do with their children. This, to some extent, exacerbates their emotional turmoil and forces them to reflect on the meaning of being a good father. Their inability to economically measure up to the "good father" image adopted by urban men, and the emotional cost of migration, made many migrant fathers in our study, although they worked very hard to support their children, still define themselves as "not a qualified father" or "as a father, not good enough." This double emotional burden puts their fatherhood in crisis.

Material Compensation and Telecommunication

To cope with the emotional turmoil or cost and reconstruct their image of a "good father," some migrant fathers resorted to compensating their left-behind children by satisfying their material needs. This coping mechanism is similar to that of migrant mothers in many studies of transnational motherhood (Hondagneu-Sotelo and Avila, 1997; Parreñas, 2001; Madianou and Miller, 2012). As Li, the twenty-five-year-old taxi driver with two young children, said,

> My elder daughter usually called me to buy something for her. I usually tried my best to satisfy whatever she asked for. Try my best to satisfy her material needs. For example, if she asks me to buy her a toy car or a book, I would buy it without hesitation.

Satisfying children's material needs echoes Chinese fathers' traditional duty: providing for their families and children. However, being a breadwinner is not enough for migrant men to construct their role as a good father. In contemporary societies, the quality of parent-child relationships is believed to largely derive from the so-called "quality time" that parents and their children spend together and the intimacy they feel for each other. As Dermott (2008: 139) pointed out, "The contemporary idea of intimacy is based on a 'dialogic ethos,'" and communication is believed to be an important channel or basis on which to form an intimate relationship. Transnational mothers use intensive telecommunication as a significant way to maintain their emotional bonds with their left-behind children (Hondagneu-Sotelo and Avila, 1997; Parreñas, 2010; Madianou and Miller, 2012). Like these transnational mothers, many migrant fathers in our study also rely on mobile phones to maintain telecommunication with their left-behind children, get information about their children's daily lives, and express their concern for their children. The penetration of mobile phones among migrant workers in China is a recent phenomenon. Before 2000, mobile phones were a luxury for migrant workers. Many fathers recalled the difficulties they experienced in making contact with their children and being an absent father. As So, a fifty-year-old cleaner from rural Guangdong and father of one son, stated,

> We left him to my parents when he was two years old in 1993. I seldom went back to visit him, less than once a year. . . . I missed him so much. I always thought about him. . . . Sometimes, we called. We went to the public phone booth to make a call. At that time, there was only one public phone in my village. When the guy [who is in charge of the public phone] answered the call, he had to run to my home to ask my parents to take the call. It was very inconvenient at that time. No mobile phone, only public landline phones. We could talk on the phone for several minutes as it charged a lot for long-distance calls.

Since the beginning of this century, mobile phones have gradually penetrated into every corner of mainland China and have become affordable communication devices for migrant workers since 2005 (Law and Peng, 2007; 2008). According to data released by the Ministry of Industry and Information Technology, from 2007 to 2012 the number of mobile phone subscribers in mainland China has doubled from five hundred million to one billion.[2] When we interviewed these migrant fathers between 2012 and 2015, all of them had mobile phones and many fathers made regular contact with family members in their native village. Kwan, a forty-one-year-old cook from Sichuan province and father of two sons, told us,

---

2. http://tech.sina.com.cn/t/2012-03-20/11476855132.shtml

I always call them [his children]. Last year, they were sick for a while. During that time, I called them every day. . . . I am not at home. I can get the information of what happened to them only through making calls. So, I call them no matter whether there is something happening or not. Although he may not be patient to talk to me when I call, I still have to do so. What if something has happened? I have to call. It makes me feel relieved.

Some fathers performed their paternal duties by exhorting their children to be careful and advising them to listen to their caregivers when they made calls. Qian, a thirty-five-year-old factory worker from Henan and father of two children, is a case in point:

Worry. I am worrying about the safety of my children. . . . There is a big reservoir near my house. I worry that my son may have accidents when he swims in the reservoir. When I call him, I always warn him and tell him not to swim in the reservoir.

Luckily for these migrant fathers, the cost of long distance calls through mobile phone has been decreasing. As Zhen, a thirty-eight-year-old migrant father of two children, stated,

Sometimes I make calls twice a day. . . . The phone bill is not high, is it? . . . [On the phone], I tell him: "Study hard. Don't be naughty. Listen to your grandpa and grandma."

Children's academic performance is an important topic in the telecommunication between migrant fathers and their children. Some migrant fathers reported that, although they were unable to supervise their children's study because of their low education level and long-term absence, they still asked about their children's study progress and academic performance and urged them to study hard on the phone. As Ai, a forty-year-old taxi driver from rural Guangdong and father of three children, stated,

I contacted my son by phone. I told him: "Spend more time on study. Study hard." I asked him: "Did you finish your homework?" He said: "I have finished it." And I asked: "Is there any unfinished homework?" He replied: "No. I have finished all my homework at school." I urge him to study hard every day.

Maintaining mobile communication can also satisfy migrant fathers' emotional needs, especially when they long for their left-behind children or encounter problems in their work. Talking to their children and other family members on the phone can cheer them up. As Fei , a migrant father of two children, told us in the interview, "Sometimes, when I feel unhappy, when I feel downhearted, I make a call to my family in my native village. Making a call, talking to them on the phone, and then I feel much better."

However, not all migrant fathers handle their emotional issues actively. Some fathers reacted very passively to the emotional distance between themselves and their children as a result of their migration and long-term absence. Neither did they put much effort into rebuilding the emotional connections with their children. As Tsang, a thirty-two-year-old carpenter from Hubei and a single father of a young son, told us,

> He [his son] lives with my mom. They are emotionally close to each other. He does not have much emotional attachment to me. He does not like being together with me. He is afraid of me. . . . I don't miss him. What should I miss him for? He is well cared for by others. He is fed by others. I sent him money. That's enough. . . . There is a huge distance between him and me. We don't have much communication with each other.

Tsang's passive reaction to his emotional disconnection with his left-behind child may derive from his lack of confidence in or knowledge about winning his son's heart from a distance. Another possible reason is that, as many scholars have indicated (Wilding, 2006; Peng and Wong, 2013), the intimacy brought by telecommunication, to some extent, exacerbated the pain caused by physical separation. Thus, just like Tsang, some fathers chose to keep an emotional distance from their children to suppress the pain caused by their long-term separation.

Changing Fathering Practice and Aspiration

The emotional factors not only feature in migrant fathers' daily contact with their children, they are reflected in the manner in which they discipline their children. In traditional Chinese societies, the father is the authority figure in his family and is responsible for regulating his children's behavior, socializing his children into modest and cooperative social members who can live in and be integrated into a collectivist society (Hsu, 1971; Wu et al., 2002). As a Chinese classic text, the *Three Character Classic* (*san zi jing*), stated, "To feed without teaching is the father's fault" (*zibujiao, fuzhiguo*). In traditional Chinese authoritarian parenting, disciplining children by beating is acceptable. As an old Chinese saying states, "Dutiful sons are the product of the rod" (*gunbang dexia chu xiaozi*). However, these traditional Chinese parenting ideologies encounter new challenges when millions of migrant men, as fathers, leave their children behind, lose daily contact with their children, and sometime even feel a lack of legitimacy in disciplining their children. Some migrant fathers reported that they transformed their discipline style, because they felt so guilty for not being able to spend time with their left-behind children and provide them with a good environment in which to grow up. Xuan, a fifty-year-old construction worker from Henan, and his wife left their two children with his mother-in-law thirteen years ago when they departed their native village to work in the cities. When his children became teenagers, Xuan found it hard to discipline them. Xuan worried that strict discipline would break the vulnerable emotional connection between them. As he said,

> It is hard to discipline my boy. My boy is a little bit naughty. We were never there for him. . . . You know, children may not understand. If you beat him, he will be angry at you. He would say: "When I grow up, I will never visit you." He would say something like this. . . . Even if he is naughty, I couldn't bear to beat him.

Although many fathers admitted that their long-term separation from their left-behind children created difficulties for them in child discipline and worried that their left-behind children may be spoiled by the grandparents who are their substitute caregivers, not all of them treated this as an insurmountable problem. Some fathers believed that they could utilize their long-term separation and physical absence in their left-behind children's lives to create a special context in which to push their children to become independent. Mai, a thirty-two-year-old construction worker from Henan and single father with a young daughter, is a case in point. Mai became a single father after he broke up with his girlfriend, who left their newborn daughter with him. He worked in a construction site in Shenzhen when we interviewed him, and left his six-year-old daughter with his parents in rural Henan. He attributed his failed relationship with his girlfriend to his low educational level and poor breadwinning capacity. He wished his daughter to have a different and better life. To help his daughter get a good job and find a good husband in the future, he believed that he needed not only to provide his daughter with good educational opportunities, but also to train her to become independent. Mai had considered bringing his daughter to Shenzhen to study. However, being a single father with a busy work schedule, he worried that he would not be able to manage the double duties of work and child care. At the time of the interview, Mai had sent his young daughter to a boarding school in their county. He believed that this was the best arrangement he could make. As he stated,

> The education service in our county is very good. In that boarding school, the school bus sends children back to their homes twice a month. They send

children back on Friday and pick them up to school next Monday. . . . Children stay at home four days a month. I believe this is good. This could teach her to live an independent life. If she [his daughter] can be independent now, when she grows up, like seventeen, eighteen years old, she will think "I can rely on myself since I have been independent for such a long time." If I brought her here [Shenzhen] to live with me, she would become dependent on me. I cannot let that happen. . . . Thus, I put her into a boarding school. . . . At the beginning, she cried because she was not used to it. After a while, she gets used to her life in the boarding school. Now, she is very independent.

As a single father, Mai said that his biggest aspiration in life was raising his daughter and giving her a good future. Mai believed that, as the father's duty, he should take care of his daughter until she gets married. Until then, he should do whatever he can to help her get a good education and have her own career. To achieve those goals, he needs to prepare at least three hundred thousand yuan for his daughter's daily expenses, her education fees, and a start-up fund for a small business if she wants to have her own business when she grows up. To save enough money, he works very hard in Shenzhen and postpones marriage. He believes that all the sacrifices he makes and the bitterness he feels will be rewarded when his daughter grows up and has a good life.

Giving their children a good life and a bright future is the common cherished goal of many migrant fathers. This is also their main motivation for migration. Migration has allowed these fathers to fulfill their provider role and support their children's growth and development. Although migrant fathers express negative feelings caused by their migration and long separation from their children, they also recognize that migration has granted them opportunities to experience some positive emotions and rewards. Migrant men feel proud, joyful, and satisfied when their children have succeeded in attending colleges, finding a good job, or establishing a family. Their children's growth and academic or career success becomes the strongest evidence for migrant fathers to prove that they have fulfilled their paternal duties. They also use their children's success to justify the emotional costs that they and their children suffered as a result of their migration and long-term separation. As three migrant fathers stated,

No matter how hard and exhausting our work is, we feel rewarded when we hear that our sons have achieved academic success [going to college]. We feel very happy about that. Having excellent sons, we feel very happy and proud. We believe that we have found the meaning of migration and our hard work.

> The happiest thing in my whole life is that I raise my children. . . . As a father, my children having a career and a family is my biggest source of happiness.

> Pride. When he [his son] studies hard and becomes the number one student in his class, I feel proud of him. He earns face for us.

To some extent, their children's success, no matter in what form, helps these migrant fathers to regain their dignity as a man and as a father in the cities in which they are treated as second-class citizens by state policy, defined as "economically unsuccessful" men because of their usually low-paid jobs, and hence looked down upon by urban citizens.

CONCLUSION

For millions of male rural-to-urban migrants in China, migration is not only the process that grants them the opportunities to increase their income and experience colorful urban lifestyles, but is also "a process that dissociates individuals from their family and friendship networks, as well as from other socially significant referents that have strong emotional connotations" (Skrbis, 2008: 236). Although overlooked or underestimated in previous discussions of migrants, emotions are constitutive parts of migrant men's experiences as family members and, more specifically for our study, as fathers. Being a migrant father in the current social context of China means making a "difficult balance between the economic benefits of migration and the emotional costs identified largely as the loss of contact with one's own children" (Skrbis, 2008: 237). Being a migrant father also involves a reconstruction or reconfiguration of one's relationship with one's left-behind children and dealing with various emotions involved in that process. Our informants shared with us their rich emotions from the migration process: their longing and nostalgia for their left-behind children, the guilt and pain caused by their separation from their children, the sorrow and frustration caused by their inability to be an economically successful father, and their pride and delight when their children achieved certain forms of success. These emotions reflect how these migrant men experience and interpret their role as fathers on the one hand, and transform their fathering practices on the other. To compensate the emotional loss caused by long-term physical separation and create an actual experience of copresence with their left-behind children, these migrant fathers rely on regular remittances, short-term visits, and telecommunication to fulfill their paternal duties and win their children's hearts from a distance. Some migrant fathers even transformed their traditional discipline styles because of their guilt toward their left-behind children. Although most migrant men worked very hard to provide for their families, especially their left-behind children, the emotional costs of their migration were so huge that the majority of them believed that the material benefits could not cure the pain suffered by both parties, and few defined themselves as "good fathers."

Migrant fathers who leave their children behind struggle to cope with the emotional cost of separation; however, migrant fathers who bring their children to the city face another set of problems. As we discussed in chapter 5, many migrant men whose young children are living in the city play a greater role in child care than is traditional, for example taking shift work in order to combine their child care responsibilities with paid work. Increasingly, migrant families with children in the city consider bringing members of the extended family, such as grandparents, to the city to provide child care. But as we will discuss in chapter 7, many grandparents are hesitant about relocating to the city, because they are not used to city life. In spite of the creativity migrant families display in devising strategies to manage the child care issue—including the behavioral adjustments made by some migrant fathers—some migrant fathers feel guilty that their children in the city do not receive adequate care. For example, a thirty-six-year-old migrant father, who worked as a full-time security guard at a karaoke bar and part-time motor taxi driver, confessed that he and his wife sometimes resorted to locking their five-year-old son in their rented room when both of them had to work and no adult was available to look after him. He recognized that locking up a five-year-old was not a good choice, but reasoned that it would at least stop his son wandering away from home unaccompanied and getting run over by a car or being kidnapped. Goodburn (2014) has also shown that, best efforts notwithstanding, rural-to-urban migrant parents with children in the city face formidable challenges in providing adequate care, because of their limited socioeconomic resources, social isolation, and migrant status.

In sum, our findings in this chapter change our stereotypical understanding of Chinese fathers, especially traditional rural fathers, who are stereotyped as unemotional, commanding, and authoritarian. The emotional turmoil experienced by these migrant fathers reveals another side to the stories of China's economic reform, mass internal migration, and grand social transformations.

CHAPTER 7

Filial Piety from Afar

Migrant Sons Renegotiating Elderly Care

Yao, a forty-five-year-old security guard who had migrated from Hunan province to work in Shenzhen, told us that his greatest regret was that for eleven consecutive years he had not been able to return home to visit his aging parents during the Spring Festival. Yao and his forty-four-year-old wife both work in Shenzhen and their twenty-one-year-old son studies at a university in Shanghai. Yao lamented that it would cost him several months' salary—his monthly wage was eighteen hundred yuan—to return home to visit his parents during the Spring Festival: transport costs would be a few hundred yuan, but he would need to spend thousands to purchase gifts for relatives. He also said his boss would not let him take leave during the Spring Festival, because if he and his security-guard colleagues returned home, there would be nobody to guard the factory. To try to make up for not being able to visit, Yao would buy clothes and food, and ask fellow Hunanese to deliver them to his parents. Yao said that his parents, who were in their early eighties, were very understanding and never complained about his absence; however other villagers had criticized him for not being a filial son. Yao repeatedly told the interviewer that he planned to return to his native village to serve his parents within two years. When asked if his wife and son supported his decision, he said,

> Even if they disagree, I am returning to [our village] in two years. I will find something to do at home, perhaps get work as a security guard in the town nearby. I would earn thirteen hundred yuan and I can look after my parents.

This is my biggest wish ... what if my parents die—if I am rich, but my parents have already died, no matter how much money I earn, it is meaningless. ... I am definitely returning home even if I have a very good job here. ... My parents could die and I would forever live in regret. ... Sons have an obligation to serve and care for their aging parents. ... I need to return, this is a matter of conscience.

Yao was apparently torn between his conflicting responsibilities toward his aging parents and his son. For him, going out to the city to *dagong* was not a choice; he saw it as the only way he could pay for his son's education and thus help him escape poverty. In order to save enough money to pay for his son's education he had for many years passed over his filial duty as a son. Yao's son was close to finishing his university education when we met, so Yao was determined to reprioritize his time and resources and return home to care for his aging parents. The decisions Yao has had to make during his migration are not easy ones. They are freighted with a complex mixture of worry, anxiety, guilt, regret, and anger. While he is living away from his parents, Yao worries about their health and safety. He is anxious about how other villagers assess him as a son. He feels guilty for not being able to be around his parents and take care of them. He fears that he will regret it for the rest of his life if he does not go back until it is too late. And he is often angry at himself for not having acted as a dedicated son before now.

Wang left his native village for city work when he was twenty years old. His wife began her *dagong* life in cities when she was nineteen years old. In their forties when we met them, they were struggling to find the money to pay the mortgage on a flat in a township near their rural home. The flat was for their thirteen-year-old son, who lived with Wang's eighty-year-old widowed mother. Wang's mother had been helping the couple by taking care of their son while they were working in the city. However, she had high blood pressure and suffered a major illness in 2013. Since then she had not been able to farm the small plot of land owned by the Wang family. She was no longer able to look after her grandson; in fact she needed care. In the end it was Wang's elder sister who left her city job and returned home to look after their frail mother.

Su is a construction worker from Hubei province who was fifty-one years old when we met him. In 2005 he left home for work in Guangzhou. His wife followed him in 2006. Their twenty-five-year-old daughter is married and was living in a village near their rural home. Their twenty-year-old son is also a migrant worker in Guangzhou. Su's elder brother and his wife and their three children all work in cities. Su's mother is eighty-one years old. Su's wife maintains that because the old lady can still wash clothes and cook, she is independent and does not need care. Now Su's married daughter is dropping by once a week to check on her grandmother; the Su family has also asked the neighbors to keep an eye on her. Su's wife felt sorry for her mother-in-law, commenting,

> She has two sons and five grandchildren. All her life she sacrificed herself for the family . . . nobody would think that with so many sons and grandchildren, at the end, she would end up living alone. When my father-in-law passed away, we were working in the city. All of us in the city. Only my mother-in-law and my father-in-law were at home. My mother-in-law went to the market to buy some food and when she returned, my father-in-law had already passed away. You see, what's the meaning of life? Such a hard life sacrificing oneself to raise two sons and five grandchildren, but when he died, he died alone. . . . Some people said that Chairman Mao's era was a better time [for old people], our time is a painful time [for them]!

The stories of Yao, Wang, and Su might lead one to think that the exodus of migrant men, which has resulted in their aging parents being left uncared for in the villages, reflects an erosion of intergenerational interdependence and reciprocity in postsocialist China, yet like most of our respondents these three placed filial piety at the heart of their ideas about manhood and womanhood when giving us their personal stories. We will argue in this chapter that what Yao, Wang, and Su's stories illustrate is not so much a fading of cultural support for the idea that adult sons have a duty to serve and care for their aging parents, but a broadening in the ways this duty is fulfilled, as well as a discrepancy between the cultural ideal of intergenerational reciprocity and what actually happens in terms of arrangements for care of the elderly since the mass migration of the young and able-bodied from rural to urban China.

Yao, Wang, and Su's stories echo national concerns about the care gap affecting rural elderly people, concerns captured in the term "hollow village" (*kongxin cun*) and more bluntly and more graphically in folk epigrams such as "Village from outside, not-village from inside, empty old houses, deserted fields, and weedy grounds" (*waimian xiangge cun, jincun bushi cun, laowu meiren zhu, huangdi zacao sheng*). This epigram vividly captures the gloom of these villages. The picture it paints of elderly men and women standing alone, holding photographs of their migrant children, or tending chickens outside their newly built big houses is a far cry from the idealized multigenerational Chinese household in which elderly family members enjoy the companionship and support of their married sons, daughters-in-law, and grandchildren. While rural men of working age have left the villages en masse to take jobs in the city, elderly people and children have remained behind. For the children this stay in the village is temporary; one day these left-behind children will pack up and follow in their parents' footsteps, embarking on a *dagong* life in the city. And when they do so their elderly grandparents are left behind in an empty-nested household. The Chinese state is grappling with the social impact of rural-to-urban migration on the well-being of these "empty-nested elderly" (*kongchao laoren*) by launching "campaigns of love toward empty-nested elderly" (*guanai kongchao laoren xingdong*). Local cadres are mobilizing resources to build care homes for the elderly that are paradoxically named "Happiness Mutual Help Communes" (*xingfu huzhu she*) to cope with the impact rural-to-urban migration has on the Chinese family.

Rural-to-urban migration has created a paradoxical intergenerational dynamic; not only has it rendered it problematic for adult men to fulfill their obligations to their aging parents, it has also meant that aging parents are called on to fill the care gap experienced by the younger generation, acting as caregivers for their grandchildren, also left behind when their sons and daughters-in-law migrate. How do male migrant workers, who are traditionally expected to be the main providers of elderly care, meet the care needs of their aging parents? How do they reconcile their cultural obligation to care for their aging parents with their inability to care for them personally owing to their long-term absence from the village? How do they cope with the paradox of having to rely on their aging parents to care for their children, when it is supposed to be them caring for their elderly parents?

This chapter provides some answers to these questions. It argues that although structural changes, such as rural-to-urban migration, pose a challenge to the Chinese family and have imposed constraints on family behavior, the core value of intergenerational interdependence has endured. We argue that the diverse strategies male migrant workers and their families use to bridge the elderly care gap represent an adaptive response to the challenge migration poses to traditional Chinese family values. Our data suggest a remarkably high level of acceptance of the norm of filial piety among male migrant workers, including the duty to serve and care for their parents in old age. There were differences between the migrant men in our sample in terms of the care strategies they had adopted, and the cultural tactics they had mobilized to rationalize the discrepancies between their beliefs and practices. Our analysis suggests that elderly care has become a flexible concept, and that previous definitions have been extended or stretched. We found evidence for the persistent rhetoric of dedicated care, and two main care strategies: collaborative care and crisis care. We also describe three processes migrant men use to rationalize the discrepancies between their beliefs and their practices with respect to care for the elderly: the family obligations of adult sons have been redefined to shift the emphasis from adult men's duty to care for their elderly parents toward their duty to provide for their offspring; the role of an adult son as a direct provider of care to aging parents has been deemphasized, and instead more stress is placed on the duty to listen to and obey their advice. Adult men compensate for their inability to provide physical care for their aging parents by offering emotional support via phone calls and occasional visits, and by providing financial support in the form of remittances during festive events. Reinterpreting the old ethos of filial piety allows male migrant workers to reconcile themselves to the economic realities of migration and balance the sometimes conflicting needs of their parents and children.

FILIAL PIETY IN POSTSOCIALIST CHINA

China's population is aging rapidly. The 2010 census showed an increase in the proportion of the population who were sixty-five or older, from 7 percent in 2000 to 9 percent in 2010 (National Bureau of Statistics of China, 2011a). China has formally become an aging society, according to the standard definition of having 7 percent of the population aged sixty-five years or older. The problems associated with an aging population, including the elderly care gap, are particularly pronounced in rural areas. Historically, rural people have been worse off than their urban counterparts, because since the Communist revolution many urban workers have had access to government pensions (Davis-Friedmann, 1983). To remedy this rural-urban inequality, the Chinese government launched the national Rural Pension Pilot Scheme in 2009 and pledged to achieve 100 percent geographical coverage by 2013. A national rural social assistance program (dibao) was rolled out in 2007 and covered close to fifty million people by 2012. The New Cooperative Medical Scheme of health insurance expanded rapidly and had achieved 95 percent coverage by 2012 (Cai et al., 2012). Despite these government initiatives, a comprehensive report published by the World Bank (Cai et al., 2012), "The Elderly and Old Age Support in Rural China," concluded pessimistically that rural people in China have not been doing well. This is because rural-to-urban migration has had a serious impact on the support available to the rural elderly population. In 1991, 70 percent of the rural elderly lived with their adult children; by 2006 this figure had dropped to 40 percent (Cai et al., 2012). Rural-to-urban migration drains villages of their economic producers and also takes away their carers. Almost 70 percent of Chinese citizens aged between eighteen and fifty work in cities and towns (National Bureau of Statistics of China, 2011b). This poses a big challenge in terms of elderly care, because the benefits elderly people in rural areas receive from the various pension and social assistance schemes are small, and they therefore remain very dependent on their adult children for support.

In traditional Chinese culture the concept of filial piety is embodied in the phrase *xiao shun*; *xiao* means "serve parents" and "take good care of parents," and *shun* means "listen to and obey parents." The doctrine of filial piety has been central to orthodox Confucianism for the past two thousand years. Children, particularly sons, are expected to provide physical care and financial support for their parents in old age (Shi, 2009; Zhan and Montgomery, 2003). Although some political struggles under Communism, such as the Anti–Lin Biao Anti-Confucius Campaign of 1973–74, attacked filial piety as anti-Communist, this particular cultural norm has endured. Family support remains the major form of care for the elderly in China. Research documenting the experiences of elderly people in rural China between 1949 and the late 1970s showed that Chinese parents knew that their children were their most reliable source of support in old age, and prepared their children "for a lifetime of mutual dependency and reciprocity" from childhood onward (Davis-Friedmann, 1983: 128–29).

However, China's economic reform has created uncertainty for this century-old doctrine and its impact on elderly care. In the introduction to a special issue of *China Quarterly* on the Chinese family, Whyte (1992) noted that the economic reform program launched in rural China in the 1980s had produced two contradictory impacts on peasant families and intergenerational relationships. On the one hand, decollectivization and the associated changes had helped to restore peasant families as a unit of production, creating new incentives for families to hold together as a nexus of economic and social exchanges.

Rural parents invested in their children's education and built houses for their sons. They also helped their married children (mostly their sons) with housework and childcare. These investments promoted intergenerational interdependence and loyalty, and legitimized parents' claims for reciprocal support in their old age. On the other hand, rural-to-urban migration resulted in prolonged separation between parents and their grown children, and meant that children were unavailable to serve and care for their parents. Whyte also suggested that by exposing migrants to Western and modern values, migration may also have weakened their acceptance of filial piety and their sense of obligation to reciprocate parental investment. Whyte challenged future researchers to collect the empirical evidence to determine the predominant effects of economic reform and the consequent internal migration. Whyte also noted that the binary approach frequently taken by scholars of filial piety in China, analyzing filial behavior either in terms of a revival of traditional values and structures or in terms of modernization, might not be adequate to capture the complex reality of intergenerational dynamics in postsocialist China.

Both survey data and ethnographic studies published since 1992 have documented the continued salience of traditional familial values, most notably the norm of filial piety, among both rural and urban residents (Deutsch, 2006; Whyte, 2003a, b). The persistence of filial norms sits uncomfortably with rapidly changing patterns in parent-child interactions, particularly in rural areas (Cheung and Kwan, 2009; Croll, 2006; Palmer and Deng, 2008; Quach and Anderson, 2008). Disputes between grown children and their elderly parents over parental support became so common in the 2000s that many local governments turned to the so-called Family Support Agreement (FSA) (*jiating shanyang xieyi*) as a solution. The concept of an FSA first emerged in the mid-1980s in a local community in Dafeng County, Jiangsu Province. It has come to be viewed as a viable means of resolving disputes about parental support between parents and adult children. By 2005 more than thirteen million rural Chinese families had signed FSAs. An FSA is a formal agreement about what support and care adult children will provide for their aging parents; it is signed by both parties and monitored by local government. It has been suggested that the government's resort to formal contracts as a means of regulating family care for the elderly is an indication that traditional morality and affective bonds are no longer strong enough to ensure that grown children will take care of their parents (Chou, 2011).[1] Research conducted in urban China suggested that living in the same household or living close together was the key to supportive relationships between elderly parents and their grown children (Unger 1993; Logan and Bian, 1999). Logan and Bian (1999), for example, reported that parents cited receiving care from their children as the most important reason for preferring coresidence over alternative living arrangments. If one accepts the premise that coresidence is critical to familial provision of care for the elderly, it follows that the migration of adult children from rural to urban China would inevitably create an elderly care gap.

Existing research on how Chinese parents and adult children in migrant families negotiate elderly care suggests that both parties are remarkably flexible, adjusting their expectations and arrangements to cope with changing family and social circumstances (Lan, 2002; Sun, 2012, 2014). Lan (2003b) found that by subcontracting elderly care work to care workers viewed as fictive kins, Taiwanese immigrants in the US were able to maintain the cultural ideal of filial piety. Sun (2012, 2014) observed that aging Taiwanese immigrants in the US resolved the tension between cultural ideals of filial piety and their practical failure to care for their elderly parents by transforming "the cultural logics of intergenerational responsibility, obligation and entitlement" (875). The question of how male rural-to-urban migrants adjust and adapt their care strategies and expectations to the circumstances created by migration is a timely and important one.

MIGRATION AND THE NEW DYNAMICS OF CARE FOR THE ELDERLY

Migration has changed the dynamic of care for the elderly in rural China. First it is important to note that cultural ideals of filial piety are still overwhelmingly supported by different generations of migrant men; indeed they are recognized by migrants as core criteria of successful

1. The FSA is not the Chinese government's first intervention in family arrangements for care of the elderly. As early as the 1970s the Communist Party made it a criminal offense, punishable by a prison term of up to five years, for adult children who refuse to provide proper care for an elderly family member (Criminal Law 1979, article 183). The Chinese Constitution (National People's Congress of the People's Republic of China, 1982), the revised Marriage Law (1980, Article 20), and Law on Protection of the Rights and Interests of Older Persons (National People's Congress of the People's Republic of China, 1996) all stipulated that adult children have a legal responsibility to support their aging parents (Leung, 1997; Sheng and Settles, 2006).

manhood and virtuous womanhood. Second, despite the cultural support for filial piety, care practices are diverse and very often deviate from the cultural ideal. Although formally it is migrant men who should shoulder most of the responsibility for caring for elderly parents, in practice it is very often women, both as daughters-in-law and as daughters, who deliver practical care. Most of the migrant men we interviewed take this gender transfer of care work for granted, and none had questioned its fairness. Furthermore, although men are expected to sacrifice themselves to serve and care for their parents, in reality few migrant men are able to meet this standard of dedicated care. The majority of our male migrant respondents had instead developed collaborative care arrangements and crisis-care plans to cope with the care needs of their parents. Third, intergenerational provision of support in migrant families is anything but equal; in most cases parents give far more support to their migrant children than vice versa. These new care dynamics may not have been caused by mass rural-to-urban migration, but they are undoubtedly being accelerated and intensified by it.

Rhetoric of Dedicated Care

None of the migrant men we interviewed questioned the cultural norm of filial piety, which stresses that adult children have a responsibility to reciprocate earlier parental support by caring for them in their old age. The sentiments expressed by Xia, a twenty-five-year-old taxi driver from rural Guangdong, are fairly typical:

> Your parents raise you, they are peasants. They raise us by doing farm work. It is not easy. After you go out for migrant work, you definitely need to reciprocate your parents.

Migrant men feel that they should take care of their aging parents, but they also expect to have their wife's unquestioning support in fulfilling this duty. In traditional Chinese society sons shoulder the moral responsibility for elderly care but daughters-in-law do most of the practical care work (Zhan and Montgomery, 2003). For example, when a man's aging parents are sick, it is his wife who is expected to nurse them. In talking about virtuous wifehood, migrant men placed most emphasis on two criteria: housekeeping skills (*chijia*) and being filial (*xiaoshun*). This latter refers directly to a wife's willingness to serve and obey her in-laws.

In reality, however, the care practices of migrant men often deviate from this cultural ideal. Although daughters in rural China are considered to have left their natal families, and as "outsiders" are not expected to shoulder the responsibility of caring for their own elderly parents, we observed that in quite a number of cases the married sisters of migrant men take care for their elderly parents. When the mother of Wang (a thirty-year-old construction worker from Henan province who works in Shenzhen) was sick, it was his elder sister who took care of her, because she lived close to the hospital. Zhu (a thirty-eight-year-old security guard from Hunan who was working in Shenzhen at the time of the interview) has one brother and four sisters. His parents helped look after his brother's and his children when they were young, but now it is one of Zhu's sisters who is the primary provider of financial support to their parents, because she runs a business and is economically better off than the other siblings. Among migrant men with no sons, expectations about the role Chinese daughters should play in caring for elderly parents have changed; these men now expect and believe that their daughters will be their source of security in their old age. For example, Han (a thirty-two-year-old construction worker from Henan who was working in Shenzhen at the time of the interview) said with confidence that he believed that his only daughter would look after him when he is old:

> I can't believe that my daughter will not look after me when I am old. I raise her and it is not possible that she would not look after me.

Migrant daughters without brothers also see it as their undisputable obligation to care for their parents in old age, even if this means they have less time and fewer resources to dedicate to caring for their in-laws. In spite of the fact that married daughters play an increasingly visible role in their parents' elderly care, migrant men with sons or brothers have continued to uphold the tradition that values sons as the primary providers of care for the elderly. To them, daughters and women remain officially second-best care providers. Ye, a forty-four-year-old security guard from Hunan, summed up this attitude:

> A family with sons would not need women to support their parents. This is how I think about it. . . . Of course if a family does not have sons, then the daughters must take on the carer's role.

Despite the above deviations, migrant men still talked about wanting to be a dedicated son. For example, Zhang, the thirty-four-year-old security guard whose story we discussed in chapter 2, believed it was a son's duty to make sure that his parents did not become exhausted or burnt out from hard farm labor. Likewise Yao, the forty-five-year-old security guard we discussed at the beginning of this chapter, argued that adult children's ability to physically serve and care for their parents, by doing things such as cooking food they like, providing personal care if they are bedridden or immobile, and taking them to the hospital if they become ill, was a barometer of filial piety. For him the physical act of caring for one's parents had a symbolic and emotional meaning that care provided by a third party could not match. Migrant men who talked about wanting to provide dedicated care to their parents saw parental health as a blessing, and viewed the time they could spend with their aging parents as beyond price. They had a sense of urgency and felt provision of care needed to be timely, since their parents were aging rapidly and might die at any time. Both Zhang and Yao reiterated time and time again their fear that if they did not return to their native village in time, they would miss the opportunity to serve their parents. Some migrant men who envisaged themselves as dedicated sons spoke about sacrificing their higher city income for a lower rural wage in order to achieve their goal of being the primary carer for their elderly parents. To these men masculinity was first and foremost defined by a man's responsibility to take good care of his family (*bajiali zuohao*), and "good care" was often construed as more than financial provision. It also meant giving practical care in person, because of the importance attached to family intimacy, happiness, and harmony, things that cannot be bought with money. However, caregiving practices often diverged from the rhetoric about dedicated care. Zhang was working in a low status, low-paying job as a security guard so that he could return frequently to his village. Zhang saw this partly in terms of duty toward his aging parents, but his wife would have preferred him to find a higher-paying job and return to their rural home less frequently. Her concession may have been related to the fact that their two young children, aged eight and four, were being cared for by Zhang's parents. The question of what will happen when Zhang's children are grown up and move to the city remains. Will Zhang still be able to persuade his wife to let him return frequently to their native village to care for his parents? This is exactly the dilemma faced by Yao, the forty-five-year-old security guard we discussed above. To us Yao reiterated his determination to give up his city job and return to his rural home to care for his parents within two years, but he had no idea how he would persuade his wife (who was also working in the city) to accept his plan.

When migrant men talk about being dedicated sons they are usually referring to a plan to return to their native village and take on a carer's role. A few migrant men, however, talked about bringing their parents to the city. This approach may not be popular among elderly parents and may also not be feasible financially for their adult children. Kwan is a fory-one-year-old cook from Shanxi province who left home to find employment in Dongguan when he was seventeen. He later returned to marry a girl from a nearby village who was introduced by relatives. After the marriage Kwan took his wife with him to work in Dongguan. Kwan's parents help to look after the couple's two sons, who were seventeen and five years old when we interviewed Kwan. He told us that his parents were frail as "candles in the wind" and that he worried about their health all the time. But he could not return to the village to care for them, because he still needed to save money for his sons' education. He had tried bringing his parents and children to the city, but it did not work out:

> My parents brought my five-year-old son to join us in the city two years ago. They brought him here for the Spring Festival family reunion. They stayed for a month but decided to return to the village. . . . They are not used to city life. Old people feel uncomfortable if they are not doing some farm work or raising some pigs, chickens. . . . Perhaps they have labored all their life and they find meaning in life through labor. . . . Of course we want to bring them to the city. But this does not seem realistic. . . . Rich city people might have a flat; we only rent a room. If they come to join us, we would need to find another room nearby. That would not be easy.

In summary, although many men aspire to realize the cultural ideal of the dedicated son, this aspiration remains largely rhetorical and is not reflected in behavior. In a quantitative study of intention to return among migrant workers in the Pearl River Delta, Tong (2015) found that although having a left-behind child was a significant positive influence on migrants' intention to return, having stay-behind elderly parents was not a significant influence in the short, medium, or longer term.

CARE STRATEGIES: COLLABORATIVE AND CRISIS CARE

Recognition that the image of the dedicated son remains largely an unrealized ideal leads to the question of how migrant sons actually practice filial piety. We have identified two caregiving strategies, which we term "collaborative caring" and "crisis caring." Collaborative care involves dividing and distributing the practical aspects of the carer's role among the family. Although the cultural norm is for the elder son and his wife to assume primary responsibility for caring for elderly parents, we found considerable variation in how the burden of care is distributed. A collaborative caring strategy is the outcome of a decision by the adult children of the family to manage their obligation to provide care in a way that reflects the specific circumstances of the family rather than being bound by cultural norms that devolve responsibility according to gender and birth order. In many families the distribution of responsibilities is often pragmatic, based on the financial situation of the siblings, their availability, and proximity. For example, in a family of six siblings (two sons and four daughters) from Hunan it was the richest, married daughter who was providing financial support to the aging parents. In a family of two sons in Henan it was impractical for the elder son to serve his parents, since he had found a wife from another province while on migration and had settled in a town close to his wife's natal home. It thus fell to the younger son, who lived nearby, to take responsibility for caring for his parents. In a family of two sons from Henan the elder son was living with and supporting their ninety-year-old grandmother, and the younger son was living with and supporting their mother (their father was deceased). In a family of three sons and one daughter the grown brothers took turns living with their aging parents, and when their mother was taken ill the second son's wife left her job in the city to return and care for her. The brothers did not expect their sister to share the burden of care, although they appreciate it when she sends their parents money during the Spring Festival. In some cases migrant men leave their wives behind to care for both the older and younger generations, but it is increasingly common for couples to migrate together. Some migrant couples try to take turns staying in the family's rural home to take care of their elderly parents and young children, but for most couples this is not feasible, because it is difficult to get leave from work. This has resulted in the emergence of the second strategy, crisis caring.

Crisis caring is based on a redefinition of the filial care obligation which acknowledges that circumstances place tight constraints on what care can realistically be provided. Migrant men who adopt this strategy operate on the basis of a much more circumscribed parental entitlement to care, which only covers parents who are very elderly (e.g. in their eighties), physically disabled, ill, or bedridden. Migrant men in this category regard their inability to care for their aging parents as an inevitable outcome of migrant work. It is not that they are not saddened by their long-term absence from their aging parents. They understand that their aging parents would like them to be around more often. But they just do not see an alternative to migrant work. Yip is a thirty-year-old from Henan who was working as a construction worker in Shenzhen when we met him in 2013. He has two children, aged ten and four, who were cared for by his parents because his wife was also working in Shenzhen. Yip has an older and a younger sister, both of whom were married when we met him. Yip told us that he and his wife had their older son in 2003 and had hesitated about having another child because of the expense. In 2008 they decided to have another child; Yip wanted a daughter, because "sons do not care for their parents after they get married. Girls are more filial than sons." To his disappointment their second child, born in 2009, was another son. Yip's preference for daughters might be a result of reflecting on his own inability to care for his parents. He told us that although he had returned to see his mother when she was ill the previous year, it was his sisters who took care of her physically, taking her nutritious food and visiting her in the hospital. At the end of the interview Yip concluded by saying that as the son, he would definitely return to care for his parents, although he did not know when that would be.

Migration and Intensified Intergenerational Inequalities

Rural-to-urban migration has intensified inequalities in the intergenerational exchange of care and support. Our data show that intergenerational support flows mainly one way, from parents to grown sons. Rural parents pay for their sons' education and build them houses. They often pay the bride price and sponsor the wedding banquet when a son gets married. Because their sons and daughters-in-law leave the village for migrant work, stay-behind elderly parents are also responsible for the farm work and care of left-behind grandchildren. When a son wants to set up his own business, it is often his elderly parents who contribute their savings as start-up capital. Some parents even work as unpaid laborers in their sons' businesses. We also found that the migrant couples we interviewed were planning their lives around their sons' family needs. For example Min and his wife, who were sixty-five and fifty-six years old respectively and worked as cleaners in Shenzhen, were delaying their decision about whether to stay in the city or return to their native village until their thirty-four-year-old son, a sales assistant in Shenzhen, had settled down:

> We are waiting for our son . . . waiting for him to find a girlfriend, to get married, to have a family. Only then can we make decisions about whether or when to return to our rural home.

Although most migrant men give their parents some financial help, this is often symbolic rather than substantive. Rather than providing regular financial support, for example, they might give their parents some money during the Spring Festival. In other incidents, the parents save the money that their sons send them and use the money to help the sons when they need help. Many of the migrant men we interviewed report that their aging parents are self-sufficient:

> As long as they have a few acres of land, they can farm and sell some produce for cash. . . . You cannot make money in the village. But it is enough for elderly people. If they are sick, they go to the doctors in the village, which costs little money and is covered by medical insurance. As long as they have food on the table, that is fine.

Elderly people living in rural areas do not need much money from their children, because living costs in villages are low; however, financial support becomes a significant issue if they fall ill. By 2012 more than 95 percent of China's population were covered by medical insurance (*yibao*) (Yip and Hsiao, 2015). However, medical insurance does not cover registration fees (*guahao fei*) and medical checkup fees (*jiancha fei*). If the hospital is a long way from the village there will also be transport and accommodation expenses for the patient and accompanying family members. These costs can easily bring financial ruin on a rural household, and so migrant men worry about their aging parents becoming seriously ill (*dabing*). They tend to be ambivalent about pooling all the family's resources to pay for an elderly parent's medical treatment under these circumstances. Many have a fatalistic and pragmatic attitude; for them a person's life is finished (*wandan*) when he or she becomes seriously ill, because the family simply cannot afford to pay for expensive medical treatment. There is an understanding that children and young people should be given priority over elderly people when family decisions about the allocation of scarce financial resources are made, simply because the older people's lives are expected to end sooner. During our fieldwork we encountered a migrant woman who went out to do migrant work because she had to earn money to cover her husband's medical costs. During research on sex workers in China the first author also encountered many cases in which a mother had turned to sex work to pay her sick child's medical costs. But in our interviews with migrant men, we have not heard of a single case in which a migrant man went out to do migrant work in order to cover an elderly parent's medical costs. While rural parents invest their whole lives in their children's futures, particularly their sons, the care they receive in return is paltry.

Many migrant men acknowledge the imbalance in intergenerational support. Le, a thirty-eight-year-old taxi driver from rural Guangdong, told us that he felt deeply indebted to his parents:

> They raised me to adulthood and I went out for migrant work. Then I had my own family, but they [his parents] still need to worry about me. . . . My father is nearly seventy years old and he still needs to do farm work. In May and June he still needs to plant the rice. I feel I owe my father a lot.

How then do migrant men such as Le reconcile the often inadequate care they give their elderly parents with the cultural ideal of filial piety to which they subscribe?

RATIONALIZING DISCREPANCIES BETWEEN IDEALS AND PRACTICES

Redrawing the Boundaries of Intergenerational Obligations

Xiong is a forty-five-year-old Henanese shoe factory worker with three children who was working in Shenzhen. His wife works in Shenzhen as well. His eldest son is a migrant worker. His seventeen-year-old daughter studies and is living with them in Shenzhen, but his youngest son lives with Xiong's parents in their native village. Like most migrant men, Xiong sees his situation not as a choice, but as the only way of making a living, and he views his inability to care for his parents as an inescapable regret:

> After we go out for work, we know nothing about what happens to our parents at home. . . . The only thing I can do is to send them money. I cannot go back to visit them except during the Spring Festival. . . . I am a 50 percent son. If they have fever or headache I would not know. The only thing I do for them is to call them occasionally. I earn so little here. So I cannot bring back a lot of money. I am not at home to serve them. They keep telling me that they do not need me at home because they are in good health. . . . I know that they want me to earn more money . . . because I need to find money to help my children.

Xiong has two sons. He is resigned to the fact that his elder son, also a migrant worker, does not save much from his salary. He also had little hope for his younger son, whom he described as an uncontrollable youth who disliked studying and only enjoyed online games. Xiong blamed himself for his sons' problems and hoped to compensate by helping them to set up their own businesses in their hometown. It appeared that Xiong did not want his sons' lives to follow the same pattern as his. By urging Xiong to stay in the city as a migrant worker and not worry about them, Xiong's parents were redefining intergenerational obligations to prioritize Xiong's responsibility to help his teenage sons over his responsibility to care for them. Reluctantly and with regret Xiong followed his parents' advice; partly because of the pressure to conform to the normative expectation that a father will provide houses for his sons and prepare them for marriage, and partly because he felt guilty about neglecting his childrearing responsibilities:

> Because my sons have always been left at home [he and his wife have been going out to do migrant work], they have not been properly cared for [by him and his wife]. It has always been their grandparents who look after them. . . . I did not stay home to educate them. I did not advise them.

The prioritization of young over old is further reflected in how productive family members allocate their time and labor. Migrant men talk about "defying death" (*pinming*) and "exerting their utmost strength" (*jinli*) to earn money through migrant work to pay for their children's education. The same assertiveness is missing when they talk about their inability to fulfill their caring obligations to their aging parents. Instead, a sense of resignation prevails, and they rationalize their shortcomings. Because going out for work has become a way of life for most adult men in rural China—and increasingly for women too—elderly parents have also gradually adjusted their expectations. Many do not expect their grown children to care for them. The older migrant men in their late fifties and early sixties that we interviewed talked about not wanting to be a burden on their adult children and not wanting to "cause trouble" (*tianmafan*) or "bother" (*mafan*) their children. They said that they continued migrant work in the city in order to save money so that they would be independent and self-sufficient in their old age.

Reinterpreting Meanings of Filial Piety

As we discussed at the beginning of this chapter, the Chinese concept of filial piety has two components, *xiao* (service to one's parents) and *shun* (listening to and obeying one's parents). When migrant men do not have the means (i.e. financial resources) or are unavailable to care for or serve their aging parents (*xiao*) in person because of their migrant work, they reinterpret the concept of filial piety in terms of past obedience to one's parents (*shun*); thus a filial son becomes one who listens to his parents' advice, does not argue with them or bring trouble on them, and relieves them of the need to worry about him. The words of Cen, a fifty-year-old construction worker from rural Guangdong, and Ji, a twenty-eight-year-old taxi driver from Hunan, illustrate this redefinition:

> I think I am not a bad son. I never argue with my parents and I do not bring them trouble. For my parents, I think I have passed as a son.

> I am a family person. I have never argued with my father or my mother. . . . I have been obedient to them since I was young. . . . I think I am absolutely obedient to them. Of course I do not want them to intervene in my private business, such as my choice of girlfriends.

Parents in rural China worry whether their sons will marry in good time. This is because marrying and raising a family continue to be critically important in defining a man's life in contemporary rural China. As So, a fifty-year-old cleaner from rural Guangdong whom we met in Shenzhen in 2013, commented,

> After a person is born, he needs to fulfill his first obligation in life [marriage]. After he gets married, he needs to have children. A man must get married otherwise he will be very lonely when he is old . . . children are a man's old-age insurance.

Quite a few of the married migrant men we interviewed said that they had always considered marriage and childrearing a burden and a source of stress. Their parents, however, have very different views. They consider marriage a stabilizing factor in their sons' lives and feel they have discharged their own familial duty (*renwu*) when their sons marry. Parents therefore urge their sons to get married when they turn twenty-two, the legal age for marriage in China. Choi, a forty-four-year-old taxi driver, got married shortly after he left the army as a result of parental pressure:

> My parents asked me to get married. I did not have a stable job. I did not want to.

Choi's parents viewed helping their son find a wife as their duty, while Choi saw obedience to his parents' wish that he should marry as part of his filial obligation to them. For him, all you need in a marriage is a partner that you can put up with (*mianqiang de guoqu*). Like Choi, Liu, a forty-two-year-old construction worker from Henan, also made an arranged marriage (*fumu baoban hunyin*) after his father rejected the girlfriend he had found for himself on migration. Liu did not seem to resent his parents' decision, despite his unhappiness in the marriage. Choi and Liu's cases were not exceptional. Nearly all married migrant men reported that they had taken their parents' views into consideration when selecting a marriage partner, perhaps giving up a romance that had developed during their migration, and returning to their rural home to marry a girl of their parents' choice, as we discussed in chapter 3. Others had obeyed their parents' wishes and had more children, despite their own worries about the financial burden an additional child would place on the family.

Because they had listened to their parents when it came to these critical life decisions, migrant men considered that they had passed as filial sons. After all, in being obedient (*shun*), they had met half the requirements for filial piety (*xiao shun*). Migrant men's reinterpretation of filial piety to emphasize obedience to their parents—which they have given— rather than providing practical care and service—which they have not been able to do—reflects the way which filial norms serve as cultural tool kits (Swidler, 1986), to be appropriated and cherry-picked by individuals to rationalize their actions under various circumstances.

Care via Mobile Phone

Research on transnational migration has documented the significant role mobile phones have played in facilitating long-distance parenting, particularly by migrant mothers with left-behind children (Peng and Wong, 2013). In our study, we observed that mobile phones played a similar role in helping migrant men take care of their elderly parents. Some migrant men used their mobile phone to monitor their elderly parents' safety and health, to give their parents instructions on domestic matters such as electrical wiring in the house, or to urge a sick parent to seek medical care and eat nutritious food. More often they use mobile phones to offer emotional care. Xiao was a fifty-year-old from rural Guangdong working as a security guard when we met him in Shenzhen in 2013. Xiao was saddened that he could not care physically for his parents, who were in their eighties:

> The only thing I can do is to call them occasionally, to ask on the phone if they are well . . . to reassure myself that they are still fine and to let them know that I am fine . . . filial piety . . . how can I explain, it is in my heart but I cannot put it into practice. My parents are already very old. If I were at home, I would cook the food that they like for them. I would chat with them. I would be able to take care of them. For example, if they were sick, I would

be able to take them to the doctor. Now I cannot do any of these things. . . . I want to be a filial son but I do not have the means to achieve this.

For Xiao the mobile phone is a means of keeping up to date about his parents' health and a way of communicating with them. It also allows his parents to follow his migrant life and relieves their worries about him. However, Xiao did not consider care via mobile phone a satisfactory substitute for being together and being able to care physically for his parents. As he continued:

> [In order to do migrant work] I have given up family happiness and opportunities to be a filial son . . . our floating life precludes family happiness. A man can only be happy if he is with his parents, wife, and children.

Migrant men like Xiao talked about elderly care via mobile phone as "the only thing I can do [for my parents]" or "the most I can do." Mobile communication technologies allowed many of them to at least get information and make certain care arrangements from a distance; however they did not feel that "caring" by mobile phone was enough. Often both parents and their adult sons will only report happy things; they hide sad news (*baoxi bu baoyou*) from each other because they do not want to give the other party an extra burden (*fudan*).

CONCLUSION

Although the cultural norm of filial piety stresses that adults sons have a duty to serve their parents, in contemporary China the reality is that many adult men have migrated from rural areas to find work and are therefore unable to meet the cultural expectation that they will care for their parents in person. They send money to their parents, but this financial support is usually symbolic. This is partly because most healthy, mobile elderly people in rural areas do farm work and can be self-sufficient. The treatment costs of an elderly parent's minor illness can be covered by medical insurance, or they can be treated in local, subsidized clinics, but treatment for a serious illness is often too expensive for a rural household to afford. If adult children do pay their elderly parents' medical bills, it is not usually the eldest son who takes responsibility; it is more common for most of the costs to be met by the richest child, or by all the children pooling their resources. Furthermore, when adult men make decisions about allocating their limited resources, their children often take priority over their parents. In summary, the support, both financial and physical, that adult sons provide for their aging parents is limited and falls far short of the ideal of filial piety.

Having said this, one should also note that migrant men in contemporary China have continued to uphold the cultural ideal of the dedicated son. Being filial has remained central to rural men's notions of manhood. Unfilial sons inevitably face criticism from fellow villagers and relatives. The question, therefore, is not whether migrant men try to care for their elderly parents, but how care is arranged and what types of care are provided. We observed two care strategies among migrant men: collaborative caring and crisis caring. The diversity in care arrangements reflects migrant men's need to adjust and compromise cultural ideals according to their family circumstances. These adjustments and compromises mean that very often elderly parents receive inadequate care. For example, migrant men pledge to return home to care for their parents, yet year after year these plans are postponed, with the result that they only manage to provide care when their elderly parents have fallen ill or become too old to be self-sufficient. This often means that even very elderly parents (those over the age of eighty), may not receive care from their adult migrant children. We identified three processes by which migrant men reconciled the care they actually provided with the cultural ideal of filial piety that they continued to endorse: redrawing the boundaries of intergenerational obligations, redefining the meanings of filial piety, and emotional support via mobile phone.

The bulk of migration research has focused on the people who move. The stories of the migrant men in this chapter highlight the impact of migration on China's millions of rural elderly and remind us that migration probably has just as much impact on those left behind.

CHAPTER 8

Masculine Compromise

*A Feminist Framework of
Changing Masculinity*

How has migration changed the Chinese family? Drawing on ethnographic materials and in-depth interviews with 192 rural-to-urban migrant men in South China, this book examines the effect of rural-to-urban migration on family and gender relationships with a specific focus on changes in men and masculinities. Specifically, it asks three pairs of questions: (1) How does migration challenge the Chinese patriarchy, and how do migrant men respond to this crisis of masculinity and the challenge it poses to male cultural supremacy in the context of love and intimacy? (2) How do men who are part of a migrant couple or migrant family negotiate marital power and the division of housework, and how do they reconcile traditional gender norms with the reality of postmigration life in the city? (3) How do migrant men cope emotionally with separation from left-behind family members, especially their young children and elderly parents, and how do they reinterpret their roles as fathers and sons in the context of family separation?

Chapter 1 explained how the book departs from previous research in three respects. First, it examines the impact of rural-to-urban migration on family dynamics and intrafamily negotiation processes rather than analyzing quantifiable outcomes and structural consequences as previous studies of the Chinese family have done. Second, it specifically considers the emotional dimension of intergenerational dynamics in migrant families and devotes considerable space to discussing individual agency in intimate relationships and conjugal negotiations. Third, it focuses on the voices and subjective experiences of male migrant workers, using a feminist perspective that recognizes gender as partly produced through interactions between men and women, thus addressing the previous neglect of migrant men's subjectivity in the migration literature.

Chapter 2 described the migration history of four men, weaving their stories through the grand narrative of China's economic modernization, and considering the role of the state in regulating migration flows through its *hukou* system and other policies. By locating personal experience within an institutional context, this chapter provides the context for the subsequent examination of how migration shapes family life, looking at the macrostructural context of rural-urban inequality, and how state and capital collude in the exploitation and marginalization of migrants in postsocialist China.

Chapter 3 explored the dating practices and intimate relationships of young migrant men. Migration gives young men the opportunity to look for partners from different regions and experience romantic love, but it is an additional source of conflict with parents who would prefer a local daughter-in-law. Influenced by the urban ideologies of romantic love and consumerism, young migrant men place more emphasis on having a spiritual connection with an intimate partner, and connect their dating practices with consumption. However, migration does not grant them total independence when it comes to decisions about marriage; because they depend on their parents to build them a marital home and pay for the wedding, they often have to compromise on their choice of marital partner. Some young men yield to economic reality and break up with the girl that they have found for themselves; instead they follow parental suggestions, falling in with their arrangements for marriage to another, often local, girl.

Chapter 4 outlined the complex dynamics of marital power negotiations resulting from and related to migration, illustrating both continuities with the traditional pattern of male dominance in marriage and changes to this pattern. Migration to cities increases disagreement between couples about postmarital living arrangements, the wife's relationship with her natal family, her participation in urban paid employment, and the husband's spending. Migrant men distinguish between "big" and "small" decisions; they strive to preserve their dominance when it comes to big decisions related to patrilineality and patrilocality, although they are forced to make compromises over the traditional gender divide between outside and inside domains. Migrant men consider it legitimate for their wife to be in charge of small decisions, including those about household finances and the men's personal spending, but in spite of this, marital conflict about the husband's spending is common, because cities are sites of consumption and are saturated with temptation. This chapter identifies four patterns in migrant men's resolution of gender conflicts in their marital relationships: delegation, communication, ostensible concession, and confrontation. It also discusses how these patterns are linked to heterogeneities in migrant men's circumstances.

Chapter 5 described how migration to the city has created novel contexts that make negotiation of housework responsibilities central to conjugal relationships and the definition of masculinity. We identify four patterns in migrant men's responses to housework and child care tasks in the postmigration household: extended exemption, strategic avoidance, selective acceptance, and active participation. Some migrant men who take on an equal or majority share of housework attempt to downplay their contribution in the domestic sphere, some have to withstand the ridicule of their peers, and some have to sacrifice their pride, accepting a low-status job that allows them to combine work and family responsibilities. For these men increased participation in domestic and care work is problematic; they legitimize it through a discourse that locates manhood in a man's loyalty to his family and responsibility to care for them. This family-oriented concept of "respectable manhood" is constructed as a counterdiscourse to the dominant urban ideals of "monied manhood" and "quality manhood." This counterdiscourse not only provides a rationale for migrant men's unconventional domestic role, it also rehabilitates them from the humiliation they experience in the cities as second-class citizens and marginalized workers, thus undercutting gender and rural/urban inequalities.

Chapter 6 examined migrant men's emotional responses to the experience of being absent fathers to their left-behind children and their diverse coping strategies. Migration has allowed these fathers to fulfill their provider role and support their children's growth and development financially. Migrant men take pride and pleasure in having been able to provide this economic support if their children succeed at college, find a good job, or establish a family; they use their children's success to justify the emotional toll migration and long-term separation has exacted on them and their children. However, they more often suffer a double emotional burden: sadness, guilt, anguish, and worry about the prolonged periods of separation from their children is combined with feelings of inadequacy, because of their inability to measure up to the urban image of the "good father." Migrant fathers use four strategies to manage this double emotional burden and compensate their children for their prolonged absence: satisfaction of their children's material needs, maintenance of contact through mobile telecommunication, refraining from exerting harsh disciplines on their children, and develop different aspirations for their children. The complex emotions expressed by the migrant fathers we interviewed refute the stereotype of the cold and distant Chinese father. The diverse strategies these fathers adopted provide evidence of their agency and the centrality of fatherhood to contemporary Chinese masculinity.

Chapter 7 discussed the multiple strategies migrant men have devised to address the incompatibility of migrant life and the obligation to care for one's elderly parents. Migration makes it difficult for adult sons to fulfill their obligation to physically care for their aging parents; it also creates a paradoxical family dynamic in which aging parents serve as caregivers for their grandchildren, taking on the caring responsibilities that would normally fall to their migrant sons and daughters-in-laws. Our data suggest that migrant men deal with the elderly care gap left by their migration through frequent utterance of the rhetoric of dedicated care, and the mobilization of collaborative and crisis care strategies. They also resolve the discrepancies between their rhetoric of dedicated care and the inadequacy of care actually provided by redefining their obligations as adult sons in three ways: shifting the emphasis from an adult man's duty of care for his elderly parents to his duty to provide for his offspring; emphasizing the adult son's duty to listen to and obey his aging parents rather than his obligation to care for them; and providing support via occasional visits, remittances, and phone calls to compensate for an inability to provide physical care. By redefining the old ethos of filial piety, male migrant workers reconcile economic necessity with their family duties and attempt to establish a balance between their sometimes conflicting obligations to their extended and nuclear families.

In summary, our findings show that migration has considerably transformed the relationships between migrant men and their lovers, spouses, children, and parents. Young and single migrant men are thrust into the tension between the persistent influence of rural parents in their grown children's marriage decisions and the increasing cultural legitimacy for individuals in urban centers to pursue love, romance, and sexual autonomy. Married migrant men have found it increasingly difficult to maintain the traditional dominance and privilege of the husband in the realms of marital decision making and domestic division of labor. Migrant men with children find it hard to handle the emotional distance between them and their left-behind children. Migrant men also need to renegotiate their traditional obligation as filial sons from afar.

THE ACADEMIC DIALOGUE

Our findings echo previous studies on migration, family, and gender in showing that migration is a pivotal event that dramatically alters family life; they also demonstrate that these changes are gendered. Migration pushes husbands and wives, along with parents and children, to renegotiate their relationships. It creates new tensions in existing gender identities and sets the stage for contesting and reinventing established concepts of masculinity and femininity. Pioneering research documented the impact of migration on gender, marriage, and sexuality in both the recipient and sending communities (Grasmuck and Pessar, 1991; Hondagneu-Sotelo, 1994; Hondagneu-Sotelo and Avila, 1997; Hirsh, 2003; Menjivar, 2000). More recently Dreby (2010) explored how international migration produced economic inequality between migrant parents and left-behind children, and gender inequality between migrant fathers and migrant mothers. Similarly, Coe (2013) examined how transnational Ghanaian migrant families are affected by global economic inequality, African cultural and historical practices, and political policies. Research carried out in the global South (Parreñas, 2010; Gamburd, 2000; Peng and Wong, 2013, 2015; Hoang, Yeoh, and Wattie, 2012; Hoang and Yeoh, 2012; Jacka, 2012; Murphy, 2014; He and Ye, 2014; Zhang and Gao, 2014) has analyzed how migrant parents, stay-behind parents, substitute carers (often grandparents), and left-behind children adapt and maintain familial relationships when separated by migration.

The strategies developed by migrant women to cope with the challenges posed by their or their husband's migration were a central theme of earlier research. For instance, the pioneering study by Hondagneu-Sotelo and Avila (1997) introduced the term "transnational mothering" to describe the alternative childrearing arrangements developed by immigrant Latina domestic workers in the US, and their redefinition of motherhood to accommodate their long physical absence from their children's lives. More recently Peng and Wong (2013) explored how new technology, such as cell phones, has helped Filipina migrants to practice transnational mothering. What these studies have shown is that migrant women actively adjust their care practices to cope with spatial separation from their children and thus maintain their central gender identity as mothers. From this perspective, changes in mothering practices are a means of ensuring that mothering remains a central facet of femininity. Parreñas (2010) argued that the migration of women and their increasing importance as breadwinners have not led to major changes in gender relationships in the families of migrant-sending societies. Research on migrant and stay-behind fathers reveals a different dynamic from that apparent in women's responses to migration; in order to preserve their masculinity the men refuse to alter their role in care or housework. Parreñas (2001) showed, for example, that stay-behind husbands refused to take over the domestic duties of emigrant wives, because they feared that to do so would undermine their masculinity. Parreñas (2008: 1057) also argued that unlike migrant mothers, migrant fathers "insist on maintaining gender-normative views of parenting" and do not usually adjust their fathering practice to manage the spatial separation from their left-behind children, resulting in an emotional distance between father and children. More recent research by Hoang, Yeoh, and Wattie (2012), however, showed that stay-behind husbands in Indonesia and Vietnam adjusted their familial role following their wife's economic migration; for example they often became their children's principal carers. The authors argued that the differences between their findings and those of earlier studies might be because "there is actually more male participation in child care and domestic work than reported" (p. 737).[1] This finding is consistent with studies by Nobles (2011), Harper and Martin (2013), and Peng and Wong (2015), which all found that stay-behind fathers played a significant role in caring for their children after their wife's migration. Looking at another aspect of care, Lin (2014) drew attention to how rural-to-urban migrant men in China renegotiate their filial responsibilities by changing how they care for their stay-behind parents.

In summary, more recent studies of men in migrant families seem to suggest that they do indeed adjust and change their care practices and domestic role to accommodate the challenges posed to family life by migration. This conclusion is consistent with our observations, which indicate that rural-to-urban migrant men in China often adjust and change their family role and alter how they interact with family members after migration. The changes in practice are surprisingly dramatic in some instances; for example, in our chapter on domestic division of labor we showed that 44 percent of migrant men who had migrated as a couple or family were active participants in housework and child care

1. Studies of families in the US have also suggested that men sometimes underreport their participation in housework in order to appear to conform to the gender-normative role expectations of men as providers and women as homemakers (Hochschild and Machung, 2012; Bourgois, 1996a).

after migration. Most rural men would find the idea of a man doing housework laughable, so this represents a seismic change in behavior. How then can we make sense of the changes in migrant men's behavior?

One of the major contributions of feminist scholarship in the past five decades has been to challenge monolithic and static models of gendered practice and identity, as well as firmly establishing gender analysis at the intersection of structural factors, interaction dynamics, and individual agency. Inspired by this scholarship, our book has explored how migrant men's masculinity is shaped by the complicated family dynamics that are both a cause and consequence of migration, as well as by the structural obstacles they encounter during migration. By exploring the impact of migration on the family from the diverse perspectives of migrant men, this book offers an account of how the Chinese patriarchal family system is produced, reproduced, challenged, and transformed by migration. It also sheds light on how migrant men's active renegotiation of multiple male identities—good lover, responsible husband, caring father, and filial son—is linked to their engagement in urban life and is critical to the maintenance of rural-urban familial networks and fulfillment of traditional family responsibilities.

Our exploration of the subjective experiences, strategies, and agency of migrant men reveals the complexity of interactions between population movement and gender stratification processes in the context of rural-urban inequalities and changes in the institution of the family in post-Mao China. Our research suggests that although men are viewed as the de facto beneficiaries of patriarchy, migrant men do adjust their caring practices and behavior within intimate relationships to cope with the challenges of migration. This adjustment is a complex process and change is uneven; preserved and adjusted behaviors and attitudes often coexist and sometimes conflict with each other. The complexity and heterogeneity of men's responses to migration led us to ask how they might be explained. We developed the concept of masculine compromise to enable us to offer a gendered account of male migrants' response, change, and agency.

MASCULINE COMPROMISE: A FEMINIST FRAMEWORK TO ANALYZE CHANGING GENDER PRACTICE AND IDENTITY

What is masculine compromise? How does the concept help us make sense of the changes in migrant men and their masculinities? The four main threads running through our analysis are the Chinese concept of masculinity, masculine compromises, the diversity of coping strategies, and emotional consequences of and responses to migration; these themes are related to differences in individual circumstances. Migration creates new contexts for family and gender negotiations, but the responses of Chinese rural-to-urban migrant men did not fit the traditional dichotomy of resistance or conformity. Migrant men insist on preserving the twin pillars of the Chinese patriarchy—patrilineal and patrilocal practices—but compromise on the traditional "men outside, women inside" gender boundary. Migration allows migrant men to fulfill their instrumental role by supporting their parents and children economically, but it produces complex emotional responses. Migrant men's narratives of filial piety and fatherhood referred to attachment, longing, sadness, guilt, disappointment, pride, satisfaction, and joy. Although discrimination, marginalization, exclusion, and bitterness were common themes in migrant men's narratives, their responses to the constraints they faced were diverse, reflecting differences in migration type, age, income, couple-relative resources, child care needs, and gender ideology. Migrant men feel, interpret, rationalize, and cope with the impact of migration on family life in postsocialist China by mobilizing gender ideology and emotional strategies, as well as negotiating in their practices as sons, fathers, husbands, lovers, rural peasants, and urban migrants. The personal is inseparably linked to—though never completely corresponds to—the interpersonal, which in turn must be located within, but can never be reduced to, the institutional.

If women bargain with patriarchy at times of rapid social change to maximize their individual autonomy and security within the system (Kandiyoti, 1988), the migrant men in our study make masculine compromises: they strive to preserve the gender boundary and their symbolic dominance within the family by making concessions on marital power and domestic division of labor, and by redefining filial piety and fatherhood. Built on past studies on masculinity, the concept of masculine compromise provides an overall theoretical frame to analyze the ways in which migration has transformed the patriarchal Chinese family, and how migrant men have interpreted and responded to these transformations.

Our concept of masculine compromise reveals how the effects of migration on family and gender relationships in postsocialist China are characterized by a combination of pragmatic adjustments and the continued salience of male gender identity and traditional ideology. On the one hand, many practices of male dominance in the Chinese family have been challenged and transformed by rural-to-urban migration. Single migrant men do not necessarily have more say than their female partners in how an intimate relationship should progress. Married migrant men have conceded considerable marital decision-making power to their spouse and some have taken up the major share of domestic labor since migrating to the cities. Migrant fathers no longer cling to the image of an authoritarian and distant disciplinarian, and they gain more opportunities to vent their emotional longing for their left-behind children. Migrant sons have come to terms with their inability to care for their aging parents. On the other hand, migrant men continue to adhere to the entrenched ideologies of patrilineality and patrilocality. They also seldom rationalize their concessions with reference to the principle of gender equality, but justify them using conventional gender markers attached to manhood. For example, migrant men explain that they do certain household chores because these are "big," "outside," and "heavy" tasks; they let their wives decide on household finance because this involves "trivial" matters; they elucidate their equal share of domestic labor in terms of men's reluctance to quarrel with women, and men's central role in maintaining family happiness and harmony. Instead of repudiating the traditional link between economic provider and strict fatherhood, migrant men reflect on the emotional dimension of fatherhood and add emotional care to its definition. Rather than challenging the exclusion and marginalization of daughters in the Confucian discourse of filial piety, migrant men reconcile their filial obligation in emotional terms.

Mass rural-to-urban migration might have brought more gender equality to families in terms of care practices, division of labor and distribution of power, but these changing practices are not matched by an equal measure of gender-equality awakening. Rural-to-urban migrant men might make compromises when their traditional dominance in the family is challenged, but these compromises are anchored in ideologies of masculinity. The concept of masculine compromise therefore captures the agency and strategies of men in negotiating their changing roles and gender identity in the family, changes ushered in by one of the most significant mass migrations currently happening in human history: rural-urban labor migration in China. The concept also encompasses the discrepancy between practices and ideas, delineates the uneven pace of structural and cultural changes, and expounds the tension exerted by these incompatibilities on individuals and families.

The concept of masculine compromise depicts the processes of change and adjustment in the family that migrant men make postmigration. It is through making these compromises that migrant men actively do trans-local "householding" (Douglass, 2012: 4) and sustain and enact family life across multiple locations. It can be argued that masculine compromises contribute to the "success" of migrant families; however, masculine compromise is currently limited. Specific masculine compromises are the product of pragmatism rather than a transformation in cultural values and ideals. This means that there is a risk that the associated improvements in gender equality may be short-lived, and there may be a reversion to more traditional and conservative gender relationships when the conditions that forced migrant men to compromise disappear. This is, however, a pessimistic analysis. One might also argue that the new patterns of behavior generated by masculine compromise may become part of individuals' "habitus" (Bourdieu, 1977) and thus have an enduring influence on gender dynamics.

Bibliography

Atkinson, Maxine P., and Stephen P. Blackwelder. 1993. "Fathering in the 20th century." *Journal of Marriage and the Family* 55 (4): 975–86.

Baey, Grace, and Brenda S. A. Yeoh. 2015. "Migration and Precarious Work: Negotiating Debt, Employment, and Livelihood Strategies amongst Bangladeshi Migrant Men Working in Singapore's Construction Industry." *Migrating out of Poverty* RPC Working Paper. http://migratingoutofpoverty.dfid.gov .uk/files/file.php?name=wp26-baey-yeoh-2015-migration-and-precarious-work.pdf&site=354

Baron, Ava. 2006. "Masculinity, the Embodied Male Worker, and the Historian's Gaze." *International Labor and Working-Class History* 69 (1): 143–60.

Boehm, Deborah. 2012. *Intimate Migrations: Gender, Family, Illegality Among Transnational Mexicans.* New York: New York University Press.

Bourdieu, Pierre. 1977. *Outline of a Theory of Practice.* Cambridge and New York: Cambridge University Press.

Bourgois, Philippe I. 1996a. *In Search of Respect: Selling Crack in El Barrio.* Cambridge: Cambridge University Press.

———. 1996b. "In Search of Masculinity: Violence, Respect and Sexuality among Puerto Rican Crack Dealers in East Harlem". British Journal of Criminology 36: 412–27.

Boyd, Monica. 1989. "Family and Personal Networks in International Migration: Recent Developments and New Agendas." *International Migration Review* 23 (3): 638–70.

Brandth, Berit, and Elin Kvande. 1998. "Masculinity and Child Care: The Reconstruction of Fathering." *The Sociological Review* 46 (2): 293–313.

Broughton, Chad. 2008. "Migration as Engendered Practice: Mexican Men, Masculinity, and Northward Migration." *Gender & Society* 22 (5): 568–89.

Cai, Fang. 2003. *Report on China's Population and Labor: Urban Poverty in Transitional China*. Beijing: Social Sciences Documentation Publishing House.

Cai, Fang, John Giles, Philip O'Keefe, and Dewen Wang. 2012. *The Elderly and Old Age Support in Rural China: Challenges and Prospects*. Washington: The World Bank.

Cai, Fang, and Meiyan Wang. 2008. "A Counterfactual Analysis on Unlimited Surplus Labor in Rural China." *China & World Economy* 16 (1): 51–65.

Castles, Stephen, and Mark J. Miller. 2003. *The Age of Migration: International Population Movements in the Modern World*. New York: Guilford Press.

Castañeda, Ernesto, and Lesley Buck. 2011. "Remittances, Transnational Parenting, and the Children Left Behind: Economic and Psychological Implications." *The Latin Americanist* 55 (4): 85–110.

Chang, Hongqin, Xiao-yuan Dong, and Fiona MacPhail. 2011. "Labor Migration and Time Use Patterns of the Left-Behind Children and Elderly in Rural China." *World Development* 39 (12): 2199–210.

Chang, Leslie T. 2008. *Factory Girls: Voices from the Heart of Modern China*. New York: Picador.

Charsley, Katharine. 2005. "Unhappy Husbands: Masculinity and Migration in Transnational Pakistani Marriages." *Journal of the Royal Anthropological Institute* 11 (1): 85–105.

Chen, Xinxin, Qiuqiong Huang, Scott Rozelle, Yaojiang Shi, and Linxiu Zhang. 2009. "Effect of Migration on Children's Educational Performance in Rural China." *Comparative Economic Studies* 51 (3): 323–43.

Cheng, Tiejun, and Mark Selden. 1994. "The Origins and Social Consequences of China's Hukou System." *China Quarterly* 139 (September): 644–68.

Cheng, Yi'En, Brenda S. A. Yeoh, and Juan Zhang. 2015. "Still 'Breadwinners' and 'Providers': Singaporean Husbands, Money and Masculinity in Transnational Marriages." *Gender, Place & Culture* 22 (6): 867–83.

Cheung, Chau-kiu, and Alex Yui-huen Kwan. 2009. "The Erosion of Filial Piety by Modernisation in Chinese Cities." *Ageing and Society* 29 (2): 179–98.

Chiang, Yi-Lin, Emily Hannum, and Grace Kao. 2015. "It's Not Just About the Money: Gender and Youth Migration from Rural China." *Chinese Sociological Review* 47 (2): 177–201.

Choi, Susanne YP, and Ping Du. 2011. *Bupingdeng Zhong De Bupingdeng: Shehui Xingbie Shijiao Xia De Zhongguo Nongmingong* [Inequalities among Inequalities: China Migrant Workers under Social and Gender Perspectives]. Occasional Paper No. 214. Hong Kong: Hong Kong Institute of Asia-Pacific Studies. (In Chinese.)

Choi, Susanne YP, and Yinni Peng. 2015. "Humanized Management? Capital and Migrant Labour in a Time of Labour Shortage in South China." *Human Relations* 68 (2): 287–304.

Chou, Rita Jing-Ann. 2011. "Filial Piety by Contract? The Emergence, Implementation, and Implications of the 'Family Support Agreement' in China." *The Gerontologist* 51 (1): 3–16.

Coe, Cati. 2013. *The Scattered Family: Parenting, African Migrants, and Global Inequality*. Chicago: University of Chicago Press.

Cohen, Deborah. 2006. "From Peasant to Worker: Migration, Masculinity, and the Making of Mexican Workers in the US." *International Labor and Working Class History* 69: 81–103.

Cohn, Carol, and Cynthia Enloe. 2003. "A Conversation with Cynthia Enloe: Feminists Look at Masculinity and the Men Who Wage War." *Signs* 28 (4): 1187–207.

Connell, Raewyn W. 1987. *Gender and Power: Society, the Person and Sexual Politics*. Sydney: Allen and Unwin.

———. 1992. "A Very Straight Gay: Masculinity, Homosexual Experience, and the Dynamics of Gender." *American Sociological Review* 57 (6): 735–51.

———. 1993. "The Big Picture: Masculinities in Recent World History." *Theory and Society* 22 (5): 597–623.

———. 1998. "Masculinities and Globalization." *Men and Masculinities* 1 (1): 3–23.

———. 2003. "Masculinities, Change and Conflict in Global Society: Thinking about the Future of Men's Studies." *Journal of Men's Studies* 11 (3): 249–66.

Connell, Raewyn W., and James W. Messerschmidt. 2005. "Hegemonic Masculinity: Rethinking the Concept." *Gender & Society* 19 (6): 829–59.

Constable, Nicole. 1997. *Maid to Order in Hong Kong: Stories of Filipina Workers*. Ithaca: Cornell University Press.

Croll, Elizabeth J. 1974. *The Women's Movement in China: A Selection of Readings, 1949–1973*. London: Anglo-Chinese Education Institute.

———. 1981. *The Politics of Marriage in Contemporary China*. New York: Cambridge University Press.

———. 1983. *Chinese Women since Mao*. London: Zed Books.

———. 1985. "Introduction: Fertility Norms and Family Size in China." *China's One Child Family Policy*, edited by Elizabeth J Croll, Delia Davin and Penny Kane, 1–36. London: Macmillan Press.

———. 1994. *From Heaven to Earth: Images and Experiences of Development in China*. London: Routledge.

———. 2006. *China's New Consumers: Social Development and Domestic Demand*. London: Routledge.

Cruz, J. Michael. 2000. "Gay Male Domestic Violence and the Pursuit of Masculinity." *Gay Masculinities*, edited by Peter M. Nardi, 66–82. Newbury Park, CA: Sage.

Davis, Deborah S. 2014. "Privatization of Marriage in Post-Socialist China." *Modern China* 40 (6): 551–77.

Davis-Friedmann, Deborah. 1983. *Long Lives: Chinese Elderly and the Communist Revolution*. Cambridge, MA: Harvard University Press.

de Beauvoir, Simone. 1952. *The Second Sex*. New York: Knopf.

de Brauw, Alan, and Scott Rozelle. 2008. "Migration and Household Investment in Rural China." *China Economic Review* 19 (2): 320–35.

Démurger, Sylvie, and Hui Xu. 2011. "Left-Behind Children and Return Decisions of Rural Migrants in China." Groupe d'Analyse et de Théorie Économique Lyon–St Étienne, Working Paper 1122.

Dermott, Esther. 2008. *Intimate Fatherhood: A Sociological Analysis*. New York: Routledge.

Deutsch, Francine M. 2006. "Filial Piety, Patrilineality, and China's One-Child Policy." *Journal of Family Issues* 27 (3): 366–89.

Douglass, Mike. 2012. "Global Householding and Social Reproduction: Migration Research, Dynamics and Public Policy in East and Southeast Asia." Asia Research Institute, National University of Singapore Working Paper Series No. 188.

Donaldson, Mike. 1993. "What Is Hegemonic Masculinity?" *Theory and Society* 22 (5): 643–57.

Donato, Katharine M., Donna Gabaccia, Jennifer Holdaway, Martin Manalansan, and Patricia R. Pessar. 2006. "A Glass Half Full? Gender in Migration Studies." *International Migration Review* 40 (1): 3–26.

Dreby, Joanna. 2010. *Divided by Borders: Mexican Migrants and Their Children.* Berkeley: University of California Press.

Du, Ping. 2011. *Jiating Yu Shenfen: Shehui Xingbie Shijiao Xia De Dangdai Zhongguo Nongmingong* [Family and Identity: Contemporary Chinese Migrant Workers in the Perspective of Gender]. Hong Kong: The Chinese University of Hong Kong. (In Chinese.)

Du, Yang, Albert Park, and Sangui Wang. 2005. "Migration and Rural Poverty in China." *Journal of Comparative Economics* 33 (4): 688–709.

Ebrey, Patricia Buckley. 1993. *Chinese Civilization: A Sourcebook.* New York and London: The Free Press.

Evans, Harriet. 2008. *The Subject of Gender: Daughters and Mothers in Urban China.* Lanham: Rowman & Littlefield.

Fan, Cindy. 2008. *China on the Move: Migration, the State, and the Household.* New York: Routledge.

Fan, Fang, Linyan Su, Mary Kay Gill, and Boris Birmaher. 2010. "Emotional and Behavioral Problems of Chinese Left-Behind Children: A Preliminary Study." *Social Psychiatry and Psychiatric Epidemiology* 45 (6): 655–64.

Farrer, James. 2002. *Opening Up: Youth Sex Culture and Market Reform in Shanghai.* Chicago and London: University of Chicago Press.

———. 2014. "Love, Sex, and Commitment: Delinking Premarital Intimacy from Marriage in Urban China." *Wives, Husbands, and Lovers: Marriage and Sexuality in Hong Kong, Taiwan, and Urban China,* edited by Deborah S. Davis and Sara L. Friedman, 62–96. Stanford, CA: Stanford University Press.

Fernández, Itziar, Pilar Carrera, Flor Sánchez, Darío Páez, and Luis Candia. 2000. "Differences between Cultures in Emotional Verbal and Nonverbal Reactions." *Psicothema* 12: 83–92.

Flippen, Chenoa A., and Emilio A. Parrado. 2015. "A Tale of Two Contexts: U.S. Migration and the Labor Force Trajectories of Mexican Women." *International Migration Review* 49 (1): 232–59.

Friedman, Sara L. 2000. "Spoken Pleasures and Dangerous Desires: Sexuality, Marriage, and the State in Rural Southeastern China." *East Asia: An International Quarterly* 18 (4): 13–39.

Gaetano, Arianne M. 2008. "Sexuality in Diasporic Space: Rural-to-Urban Migrant Women Negotiating Gender and Marriage in Contemporary China." *Gender, Place & Culture: A Journal of Feminist Geography* 15 (6): 629–45.

Gaetano, Arianne M., and Tamara Jacka. 2004. *On the Move: Women and Rural-to-Urban Migration in Contemporary China.* New York: Columbia University Press.

Gallin, Rita S. 1994. "The Intersection of Class and Age: Mother-in-Law/Daughter-in-Law Relations in Rural Taiwan." *Journal of Cross-Cultural Gerontology,* 9 (2): 127–40.

Gamburd, Michele Ruth. 2000. *The Kitchen Spoon's Handle: Transnationalism and Sri Lanka's Migrant Housemaids.* Ithaca and London: Cornell University Press.

Gao, Qiang, and Haiming Jia. 2007. "Nongmingong Huiliu de Yuanyin ji Yingxiang Fenxi [Analysis on the causes and impact of return migrants]." *Management of Agricultural Science and Technology (Nongyekeji guanli),* 26 (4): 66–68. (In Chinese.)

Gao, Yang, Li Ping Li, Jean Hee Kim, Nathan Congdon, Joseph Lau, and Sian Griffiths. 2010. "The Impact of Parental Migration on Health Status and Health Behaviours among Left Behind Adolescent School Children in China." *BMC Public Health* 10: 56. http://www.biomedcentral.com/1471-2458/10/56

Giddens, Anthony. 1991. *Modernity and Self-Identity: Self and Society in the Late Modern Age.* Cambridge, UK: Polity Press.

Giles, John, Dewen Wang, and Changbao Zhao. 2010. "Can China's Rural Elderly Count on Support from Adult Children? Implications of Rural-to-Urban Migration." *Journal of Population Ageing* 3 (3): 183–204.

Gilmartin, Christina K., Gail Hershatter, Lisa Rofel, and Tyrene White. 1994. *Engendering China: Women, Culture, and the State.* Cambridge, MA: Harvard University Press.

Goffman, Erving. 1977. "The Arrangement between the Sexes." *Theory and Society,* 4 (3): 301–31.

Goodburn, Charlotte. 2009. "Learning from Migrant Education: A Case Study of the Schooling of Rural Migrant Children in Beijing." *International Journal of Educational Development* 29 (5): 495–504.

———. 2014. "Rural–Urban Migration and Gender Disparities in Child Healthcare in China and India." *Development and Change* 45 (4): 631–55.

Goody, Jack. 1990. *The Oriental, the Ancient, and the Primitive: Systems of Marriage and the Family in the Pre-Industrial Societies of Eurasia.* Cambridge: Cambridge University Press.

Grasmuck, Sherri, and Patricia R. Pessar. 1991. *Between Two Islands: Dominican International Migration.* Berkeley and Los Angeles, CA: University of California Press.

Guo, Man, Maria P. Aranda, and Meril Silverstein. 2009. "The Impact of Out-Migration on the Inter-Generational Support and Psychological Wellbeing of Older Adults in Rural China." *Aging and Society,* 29 (7): 1085–104.

Hagan, Jacqueline Maria. 1998. "Social Networks, Gender, and Immigrant Incorporation: Resources and Constraints." *American Sociological Review* 63 (1): 55–67.

Harper, Scott E., and Alan M. Martin. 2013. "Transnational Migratory Labor and Filipino Fathers: How Families are Affected When Men Work Abroad." *Journal of Family Issues* 34 (2): 270–90.

Harrell, Stevan. 1993. "Geography, Demography, and Family Composition in Three Southwestern Villages." *Chinese Families in the Post-Mao Era (Studies on China)*, edited by Deborah Davis and Stevan Harrell, 77–102. Berkeley and Los Angeles, CA: University of California Press.

He, Congzhi, and Jingzhong Ye. 2014. "Lonely Sunsets: Impacts of Rural-Urban Migration on the Left-Behind Elderly in Rural China." *Population, Space and Place* 20 (4): 352–69.

Heron, Craig. 2006. "Boys Will Be Boys: Working-Class Masculinities in the Age of Mass Production." *International Labor and Working-Class History* 69 (1): 6–34.

Hershatter, Gail. 2004. "State of the Field: Women in China's Long Twentieth Century." *The Journal of Asian Studies* 63 (4): 991–1065.

Hirsch, Jennifer. 2003. *A Courtship after Marriage: Sexuality and Love in Mexican Transnational Families*. Berkeley and Los Angeles, CA: University of California Press.

Ho, David Y.F. 1989. "Continuity and Variation in Chinese Patterns of Socialization." *Journal of Marriage and Family* 51 (1): 149–63.

Hoang, Lan Anh, and Brenda S.A. Yeoh. 2011. "Breadwinning Wives and 'Left-Behind' Husbands: Men and Masculinities in the Vietnamese Transnational Family." *Gender & Society* 25 (6): 717–39.

———. 2012. "Sustaining Families across Transnational Spaces: Vietnamese Migrant Parents and their Left-Behind Children." *Asian Studies Review* 36 (3): 307–25.

Hoang, Lan Anh, Brenda S.A. Yeoh, and Anna Marie Wattie. 2012. "Transnational Labour Migration and the Politics of Care in the Southeast Asian Family." *Geoforum* 43 (4): 733–40.

Holroyd, Eleanor. 2003. "Chinese Cultural Influences on Parental Caregiving Obligations toward Children with Disabilities." *Qualitative Health Research* 13 (1): 4–19.

Hondagneu–Sotelo, Pierrette. 1994. *Gendered Transitions: Mexican Experiences of Immigration*. Berkeley and Los Angeles, CA: University of California Press.

———. 2001. *Doméstica: Immigrant Workers Cleaning and Caring in the Shadows of Affluence*. Berkeley, Los Angeles, and London: University of California Press.

———. 2014. *Paradise Transplanted: Migration and the Making of California Gardens*. Berkeley: University of California Press.

Hondagneu-Sotelo, Pierrette, and Ernestine Avila. 1997. "'I'm Here, but I'm There': The Meanings of Latina Transnational Motherhood." *Gender & Society* 11 (5): 548–71.

Honig, Emily. 2003. "Socialist Sex: The Cultural Revolution Revisited." *Modern China* 29 (2): 143–75.

Hochschild, Arlie Russell, and Anne Machung. 2012. *The Second Shift: Working Families and the Revolution at Home*. London: Penguin Books.

Hsu, Francis L. K. 1971. *Under the Ancestors' Shadow: Kinship, Personality, and Social Mobility in China*. Stanford, CA: Stanford University Press.

Hu, Feng, Zhaoyuan Xu, and Yuyu Chen. 2011. "Circular Migration or Permanent Stay? Evidence from China's Rural-Urban Migration." *China Economic Review* 22 (1): 64–74.

Huang, Ping, and Shaohua Zhan. 2008. "Migrant Workers' Remittances and Rural Development in China." In Migration and Development Within and Across Borders, International Organization for Migration and Social Science Research Council Conference, November 17–19.

Jacka, Tamara. 2006. *Rural Women in Urban China: Gender, Migration, and Social Change*. Armonk, NY: M. E. Sharpe.

———. 2012. "Migration, Householding and the Well-Being of Left-Behind Women in Rural Ningxia." *The China Journal* 67 (1): 1–21.

Jacka, Tamara, Andrew B. Kipnis, and Sally Sargeson. 2013. *Contemporary China: Society and Social Change*. Port Melbourne: Cambridge University Press.

Jankowiak, William. 1993. *Sex, Death, and Hierarchy in a Chinese City: An Anthropological Account*. New York: Columbia University Press.

———. 2006. "Gender, Power, and the Denial of Intimacy in Chinese Studies and Beyond." *Reviews in Anthropology* 35 (4): 305–23.

———. 2011. "The Han Chinese Family: The Realignment of Parenting Ideals, Sentiments, and Practices." *Women and Gender in Contemporary Chinese Societies: Beyond Han Patriarchy*, edited by Shanshan Du and Ya-chen Chen, 109–32. Lanham, MD: Lexington.

Jeffreys, Elaine. 2006. *Sex and Sexuality in China*. London and New York: Routledge.

Jia, Zhaobao, and Wenhua Tian. 2010. "Loneliness of Left-Behind Children: A Cross-Sectional Survey Sample of Rural China." *Child: Care, Health and Development* 36 (6): 812–17.

Judd, Ellen R. 1994. *Gender and Power in Rural North China*. Stanford, CA: Stanford University Press.

Kandiyoti, Deniz. 1988. "Bargaining with Patriarchy." *Gender & Society* 2 (3): 274–90.

Kimmel, Michael S. 2005. "Globalization and its Mal(e)Contents: The Gendered Moral and Political Economy of Terrorism." *Handbook of Studies on Men and Masculinities*, edited by Michael S. Kimmel, Jeff Hearn, and Raewyn Connell, 414–32. London: Sage.

Kimmel, Michael S., Jeff Hearn, and Raewyn Connell. 2005. *Handbook of Studies on Men & Masculinities*. London: Sage.

Kimmel, Michael S., and Michael A. Messner. 2010. *Men's Lives*. Boston: Allyn & Bacon.

Lan, Pei-Chia. 2002. "Subcontracting Filial Piety: Elderly Care In Ethnic Chinese Immigrant Families in California." *Journal of Family Issues* 23 (7): 812–835.

———. 2003. "Among Women: Migrant Domestics and Their Taiwanese Employers across Generations." *Global Woman: Nannies, Maids, and Sex Workers in the New Economy*, edited by Barbara Ehrenreich and Arlie Russell Hochschild, 169–89. New York: Metropolitan Books.

———. 2006. *Global Cinderellas: Migrant Domestics and Newly Rich Employers in Taiwan*. Durham, NC: Duke University Press.

———. 2014. "Segmented Incorporation: The Second Generation of Rural Migrants in Shanghai." *China Quarterly* 217 (Mar): 243–65.

Lavely, William. 1991. "Marriage and Mobility under Rural Collectivism." *Marriage and Inequality in Chinese Society*, edited by Rubie Watson and Patricia Buckley Ebrey, 286–312. Berkeley and Los Angeles, CA: University of California Press.

Law, Pui Lam, and Yinni Peng. 2007. "Cellphones and the Social Lives of Migrant Workers in Southern China." *The Social Construction and Usage of Communication Technologies: Asian and European Experiences*, edited by Raul Pertierra. Diliman, 126–42. Quezon City: The University of the Philippines Press.

———. 2008. "Mobile Networks: Migrant Workers in Southern China." *Handbook of Mobile Communication Studies*, edited by James E. Katz, 55–64. Cambridge: MIT Press.

Lee, Ching Kwan. 1998. *Gender and the South China Miracle: Two Worlds of Factory Women*. Berkeley and Los Angeles, CA: University of California Press.

Lee, Deborah. 1997. "Interviewing Men: Vulnerabilities and Dilemmas." *Women's Study International Forum* 20 (4): 553–64.

Lee, Ming-Hsuan. 2011. "Migration and Children's Welfare in China: The Schooling and Health of Children Left Behind." *The Journal of Developing Areas* 44 (2): 165–82.

Leung, Joe. 1997. "Family Support for the Elderly in China: Issues and Challenges." *Journal of Aging & Social Policy* 9 (3): 87–101.

Lewis, Nathaniel M. 2014. "Rupture, Resilience, and Risk: Relationships between Mental Health and Migration among Gay-Identified Men in North America." *Health & Place* 27 (May): 212–19.

Li, Shi. 2008. "Rural Migrant Workers in China: Scenario, Challenges and Public Policy." Working Paper No. 89, Policy Integration and Statistics Department, International Labour Office. http://www.ilo.org/wcmsp5/groups/public/---dgreports/---integration/documents/publication/wcms_097744.pdf

Li, Ying, and Ernest Chui. 2011. "China's Policy on Rural-Urban Migrants and Urban Social Harmony." *Asian Social Science* 7 (7): 12–22.

Liang, Zai, Lin Guo, and Charles Chengrong Duan. 2008. "Migration and the Well-Being of Children in China." *Yale-China Health Journal* 5: 25–46.

Lin, Nan, and Yanjie Bian. 1991. "Getting Ahead in Urban China." *American Journal of Sociology* 97 (3): 657–88.

Lin, Xiaodong. 2013. *Gender, Modernity and Male Migrant Workers in China: Becoming a "Modern" Man*. London: Routledge.

———. 2014. "'Filial Son', the Family and Identity Formation among Male Migrant Workers in Urban China." *Gender, Place & Culture: A Journal of Feminist Geography* 21 (6): 717–32.

Liu, Zhengkui, Xinying Li, and Xiaojia Ge. 2009. "Left Too Early: The Effects of Age at Separation from Parents on Chinese Rural Children's Symptoms of Anxiety and Depression." *American Journal of Public Health* 99 (11): 2049–54.

Logan, John R., and Fuqin Bian. 1999. "Family Values and Coresidence with Married Children in Urban China." *Social Forces* 77 (4): 1253–82.

Loyalka, Michelle. 2012. *Eating Bitterness: Stories from the Front Lines of China's Great Urban Migration*. Berkeley and Los Angeles, CA: University of California Press.

Lu, Sheldon H. 2000. "Soap Opera in China: The Transnational Politics of Visuality, Sexuality, and Masculinity." *Cinema Journal* 40 (1): 25–47.

Lu, Feng. 2012. "Zhongguo Nongmingong Gongzi Zoushi: 1979–2010" [Wage Trends among Chinese Migrant Workers: 1979–2010]. *Social Sciences in China* 7: 47–67. (In Chinese.)

Lusher, Dean, and Garry Robins. 2009. "Hegemonic and Other Masculinities in Local Social Contexts." *Men and Masculinities* 11 (4): 387–423.

Ma, Eric, and Hau Ling 'Helen' Cheng. 2005. "'Naked' Bodies: Experimenting with Intimate Relations among Migrant Workers in South China." *International Journal of Cultural Studies* 8 (3): 307–28.

Mahler, Sarah J., and Patricia R. Pessar. 2006. "Gender Matters: Ethnographers Bring Gender from the Periphery toward the Core of Migration Studies." *International Migration Review*, 40 (1): 27–63.

Madianou, Mirca, and Daniel Miller. 2012. *Migration and New Media: Transnational Families and Polymedia*. New York: Routledge.

Mann, Susan L. 2011. *Gender and Sexuality in Modern Chinese History*. New York: Cambridge University Press.

McCoyer, Michael. 2006. "'Rough Mens' in "the Toughest Places I Ever Seen": The Construction and Ramifications of Black Masculine Identity in the Mississippi Delta's Levee Camps, 1900–1935." *International Labor and Working-Class History* 69 (1): 57–80.

Menjívar, Cecilia. 2000. *Fragmented Ties: Salvadoran Immigrant Networks in North America*. Berkeley: University of California Press.

Montes, Veronica. 2013. "The Role of Emotions in the Construction of Masculinity: Guatemalan Migrant Men, Transnational Migration, and Family Relations." *Gender & Society* 27 (4): 469–90.

Moore, Susan M., and C. Leung. 2001. "Romantic Beliefs, Styles, and Relationships among Young People from Chinese, Southern European, and Anglo-Australian Backgrounds." *Asian Journal of Social Psychology* 4 (1): 53–68.

Morokvasic, Mirjana. 1984. "Birds of Passage are Also Women." *International Migration Review* 18 (4): 886–907.

Murphy, Rachel. 2002. *How Migrant Labour is Changing Rural China*. Cambridge, UK: Cambridge University Press.

———. 2014. "School and Study in the Lives of Children in Migrant Families: A View from Rural Jiangxi, China." *Development and Change* 45 (1): 29–51.

Murphy, Rachel, Ran Tao, and Xi Lu. 2011. "Son Preference in Rural China: Patrilineal Families and Socio-Economic Change." *Population and Development Review* 37 (4): 665–90.

Mutchler, Matt G. 2000. "Seeking Sexual Lives: Gay Youth and Masculinity Tensions." *Gay Masculinities*, edited by Peter M. Nardi, 12–43. Thousand Oaks, CA: Sage.

Myerson, Rebecca, Yubo Hou, Huizhen Tang, Ying Cheng, Yan Wang, and Zhuxuan Ye. 2010. "Home and Away: Chinese Migrant Workers between Two Worlds." *Sociological Review* 58 (1): 26–44.

Nardi, Peter M. 2000. "'Anything for a Sis, Mary': An Introduction to Gay Masculinities." *Gay Masculinities*, edited by Peter M. Nardi, 1–10. Thousand Oaks, CA: Sage.

National Bureau of Statistics of the People's Republic of China. 2007. *China Rural Statistics Yearbook*. Beijing: China Statistics Press.

———. 2011a. *2010 Population Census*. Beijing: China Statistics Press.

———. 2011b. *China Statistical Yearbook 2011*. Beijing: China Statistics Press.

———. 2013. "2012 National Survey of Migrant Workers in China." http://www.stats.gov.cn/tjsj/zxfb/201305/t20130527_12978.html

———. 2014. "Report on Migrant Workers in Mainland China." http://www.stats.gov.cn/tjsj/zxfb/201405/t20140512_551585.html

National People's Congress of the People's Republic of China. 1979. *Criminal Law of the People's Republic of China*.

———. 1980. *The Marriage Law*.

———. 1982. *The Chinese Constitution*.

———. 1996. *Law on Protection of the Rights and Interests of Older Persons*.

Ngok, Kinglun. 2008. "The Changes of Chinese Labour Policy and Labour Legislation in the Context of Market Transition." *International Labour and Working-Class History* 73 (1): 45–64.

Nobles, Jenna. 2011. "Parenting from Abroad: Migration, Nonresident Father Involvement, and Children's Education in Mexico." *Journal of Marriage and Family* 73 (4): 729–46.

Ong, Aihwa. 1987. "*Spirit of Resistance and Capitalist Discipline Book*" *Spirits of Resistance and Capitalist Discipline: Factory Women in Malaysia*. Albany: State University of New York Press.

Osella, Filippo, and Caroline Osella. 2000. *Social Mobility in Kerala: Modernity and Identity in Conflict*. London: Pluto Press.

Palmer, Edward and Quheng Deng. 2008. "What Has Economic Transition Meant for the Well-Being of the Elderly in China." *Inequality and Public Policy in Urban China*, edited by Björn A. Gustafsson, Li Shi, and Terry Sicular, 182–203. New York: Cambridge University Press.

Pang, Lihua, Alan de Brauw, and Scott Rozelle. 2004. "Working until Dropping: Employment Behavior of the Elderly in Rural China." *Department of Economics Working Papers* No. 2004–14. Williamstown, MA: Williams College.

Parreñas, Rhacel Salazar. 2001. "Mothering from a Distance: Emotions, Gender, and Intergenerational Relations in Filipino Transnational Families." *Feminist Studies* 27 (2): 361–90.

———. 2008. "Transnational Fathering: Gendered Conflicts, Distant Disciplining and Emotional Gaps." *Journal of Ethnic and Migration Studies*, 34 (7): 1057–72.

———. 2010. Transnational Mothering: A Source of Gender Conflicts in the Family. *University of North Carolina Law Review*, 88 (5): 1825–56.

Peng, Xizhe. 2011. "China's Demographic History and Future Challenges." *Science* 333 (6042): 581–87.

Peng, Yinni, and Odalia M. H. Wong. 2013. "Diversified Transnational Mothering via Telecommunication: Intensive, Collaborative, and Passive." *Gender & Society* 27 (4): 491–513.

———. 2015. "Who Takes Care of My Left-Behind Children? Migrant Mothers and Caregivers in Transnational Child Care." *Journal of Family Issues* Dio:10.1177/01925X15578006

Peng, Yinni, and Susanne YP Choi. 2013. "Production Regimes and Mobile Phone Usage among Migrant Factory Workers in South China: Technologies of Power and Resistance." *China Quarterly* 215 (September): 553–71.

Phizacklea, Annie. 2003. "Transnationalism, Gender and Global Workers." *Crossing Borders and Shifting Boundaries: Gender on the Move*, vol. 1, edited by Morokvasic-Müller, Mirjana, Umut Erel, and Kyoko Shinozaki, 79–100. Opladen: Leske and Budrich.

Pun, Ngai. 2005a. "Global Production, Company Codes of Conduct and Labor Conditions in China: A Case Study of Two Factories." *The China Journal* 54: 101–13.

———. 2005b. *Made in China: Women Factory Workers in a Global Workplace*. Durham, NC, and Hong Kong: Duke University Press and Hong Kong University Press.

Pun, Ngai, and Huilin Lu. 2010a. "Neoliberalism, Urbanism and the Plight of Construction Workers in China." *World Review of Political Economy* 1 (1): 127–41.

———. 2010b. "Unfinished Proletarianization: Self, Anger, and Class Action among the Second Generation of Peasant-Workers in Present-Day China." *Modern China* 36 (5): 493–519.

Qin, Hua. 2010. "Rural-to-Urban Labor Migration, Household Livelihoods, and the Rural Environment in Chongqing Municipality, Southwest China." *Human Ecology: An Interdisciplinary Journal* 38 (5): 675–90.

Qin, Jiang, and Björn Albin. 2010. "The Mental Health of Children Left Behind in Rural China by Migrating Parents: A Literature Review." *Journal of Public Mental Health* 9 (3): 4–16.

Quach, Andrew S. and Elaine A. Anderson. 2008. "Implications of China's Open-Door Policy for Families: A Family Impact Analysis." *Journal of Family Issues* 29 (8): 1089–103.

Schmalzbauer, Leah. 2015. "Temporary and Transnational: Gender and Emotion in the Lives of Mexican Guest Worker Fathers." *Ethnic and Racial Studies* 38 (2): 211–26.

Selden, Mark. 1993. "Family Strategies and Structures in Rural North China." *Chinese Families in the Post-Mao Era*, edited by Deborah Davis, and Stevan Harrell, 139–64. Berkeley and Los Angeles, CA: University of California Press.

Sheng, Xuewen. 2005. "Chinese Families." *Handbook of World Families*, edited by Bert N. Adams and Jan Trost, 99–128. Thousand Oaks, CA: Sage Publications.

Sheng, Xuewen, and Barbara H. Settles. 2006. "Intergenerational Relationships and Elderly Care in China: A Global Perspective." *Current Sociology* 54 (2): 293–313.

Shi, Lihong. 2009. "'Little Quilted Vests to Warm Parents' Hearts': Redefining the Gendered Practice of Filial Piety in Rural North-Eastern China." *China Quarterly* 198 (June): 348–63.

Skrbis, Zlatko. 2008. "Transnational Families: Theorising Migration, Emotions and Belonging." *Journal of Intercultural Studies* 29 (3): 231–46.

Smith, Christopher J., and Xiushi Yang. 2005. "Examining the Connection between Temporary Migration and the Spread of STDs and HIV/AIDS in China." *The China Review* 5 (1): 111–39.

Smith, Robert C. 2006. *Mexican New York: Transnational Lives of New Immigrants*. Berkeley: University of California Press.

Solinger, Dorothy J. 1999. *Contesting Citizenship in Urban China: Peasant Migrants, the State, and the Logic of the Market*. Berkeley: University of California Press.

Song, Yan, Yves Zenou, and Chengri Ding. 2008. "Let's Not Throw the Baby Out with the Bath Water: The Role of Urban Villages in Housing Rural Migrants in China." *Urban Studies* 45 (2): 313–30.

Stacey, Judith. 1983. *Patriarchy and Socialist Revolution in China*. Berkeley: University of California Press.

Sun, Ken C. Y. 2012. "Fashioning Reciprocal Norms of Elder Care: A Case of Immigrants in the United States and their Parents in Taiwan." *Journal of Family Issues* 33 (9): 1240–71.

———. 2014. "Reconfigured Reciprocity: How Aging Taiwanese Immigrants Transform Cultural Logics of Elder Care." *Journal of Marriage and Family* 76 (4): 875–89.

Swidler, Ann. 1986. "Culture in Action: Symbols and Strategies." *American Sociological Review* 51 (2): 273–86.

Taylor, J. Edward, Scott Rozelle, and Alan de Brauw. 2003. "Migration and Incomes in Source Communities: A New Economics of Migration Perspective from China." *Economic Development and Cultural Change* 52 (1): 75–101.

The Ministry of Education of the People's Republic of China. 2011. "2011 Nian Zhongguo Jiaoyu Fazhan Gongbao" [The Public Report of Education Development in China in 2011]. http://www.moe.edu.cn/publicfiles /business/htmlfiles/moe/moe_633/201208/141305.html (In Chinese.)

Tong, Yuying. 2015. "Perceived Discrimination of Rural-to-Urban Migrants and Intention of Return: The Case of Pearl River Delta of China." Paper presented at the International Conference on Migration and Identity: Perspectives from Asia, Europe and North America. The Chinese University of Hong Kong, March 6–7.

Unger, Jonathan. 1993. "Urban Families in the Eighties: An Analysis of Chinese Surveys." *Chinese Families in the Post-Mao Era (Studies on China)*, edited by Deborah Davis and Stevan Harrell, 25–49. Berkeley: University of California Press.

Uretsky, Elanah. 2008. "Mobile Men with Money: The Socio-Cultural and Politico-Economic Context of 'High-Risk' Behavior Among Wealthy Businessmen and Government Officials in Urban China." *Culture, Health & Sexuality* 10 (8): 801–14.

Walter, Nicholas, Philippe Bourgois, and H. Margarita Loinaz. 2004. "Masculinity and Undocumented Labor Migration: Injured Latino Day Laborers in San Francisco." *Social Science & Medicine* 59 (6): 1159–68.

Wang, Chunguang. 2001. "Xinshengdai Nongcun Liudongrenkou De Shehui Rentong Yu Chengxiang Ronghe De Guanxi" [The Social Identification of the New Generation of Migrant Workers and its Relationship with City-Village Merger]. *Sociological Research* 3: 63–76. (In Chinese.)

Wang, Chunlei. 2013. "Woguo Nongmingong Zhengce Quxiang De Yanbian Licheng [The Policy Changes on Migrant Workers in China]." *Commercial and Economic Research* 17. http://www.ectime.com.cn/Emag.aspx?titleid = 24435. (In Chinese.)

Ward, Barbara E. 1989. *Through Other Eyes: An Anthropologist's View of Hong Kong.* Hong Kong: The Chinese University Press.

Watson, Rubie S. 1985. *Inequality among Brothers: Class and Kinship in South China.* New York: Cambridge University Press.

Wen, Ming, and Danhua Lin. 2012. "Child Development in Rural China: Children Left Behind by Their Migrant Parents and Children of Non-Migrant Families." *Child Development* 83 (1): 120–36.

West, Candace, and Don H. Zimmerman. 1987. "Doing Gender." *Gender & Society* 1 (2): 125–51.

Whyte, Martin King. 1992. "A Symposium on Rural Family Change, Introduction: Rural Economic Reforms and Chinese Family Patterns". *China Quarterly*: 130 (June): 317–22.

———. 2003a. "China's Revolutions and Intergenerational Relations." *China's Revolutions and Intergenerational Relations,* edited by Martin King Whyte, 3–30. Ann Arbor: University of Michigan Center for Chinese Studies.

———. 2003b. "The Persistence of Family Obligations in Baoding." *China's Revolutions and Intergenerational Relations,* edited by Martin King Whyte, 85–120. Ann Arbor: University of Michigan Center for Chinese Studies.

———. 2010. *One Country, Two Societies: Rural-Urban Inequality in Contemporary China.* Cambridge, MA: Harvard University Press.

Wilding, Raelene. 2006. "Virtual Intimacies? Families Communicating across Transnational Contexts." *Global Networks* 6 (2): 125–42.

Wolf, Arthur P., and Chieh-shan Huang. 1980. *Marriage and Adoption in China, 1845–1945.* Stanford, CA: Stanford University Press.

Wolf, Margery. 1968. *The House of Lim: A Study of a Chinese Family.* Englewood Cliffs, New Jersey: Prentice Hall.

———. 1972. *Women and the Family in Rural Taiwan.* Stanford, CA: Stanford University Press.

———. 1985. *Revolution Postponed: Women in Contemporary China.* Stanford, CA: Stanford University Press.

Wong, Daniel Fu Keung, Chang Ying Li, and He Xue Song. 2007. "Rural Migrant Workers in Urban China: Living a Marginalised Life." *International Journal of Social Welfare* 16 (1): 32–40.

Wong, Linda. 1994. "China's Urban Migrants—The Public Policy Challenge." *Pacific Affairs* 67 (3): 335–56.

Wu, Peixia, Clyde C. Robinson, Chongming Yang, Craig H. Hart, Susanne F. Olsen, Christin L. Porter, Shenghua Jin, Jianzhong Wo, and Xinzi Wu. 2002.

"Similarities and Differences in Mothers' Parenting of Preschoolers in China and the United States." *International Journal of Behavioral Development* 26 (6): 481–91.

Wu, Qiaobing. 2014. "Effects of social capital in multiple contexts on the psychosocial adjustment of Chinese migrant children." *Youth and Society* (online publication first).

Wu, Qiaobing, Bill Tsang, and Holly Ming. 2014. "Social capital, family support, resilience and educational outcomes of Chinese migrant children." *British Journal of Social Work* 44(3): 636–56.

Wu, Xiaogang, and Donald J. Treiman. 2007. "Inequality and Equality under Chinese Socialism: The Hukou System and Intergenerational Occupational Mobility." *American Journal of Sociology* 113 (2): 415–45.

Xiang, Biao. 2007. "How Far are the Left-Behind Left Behind? A Preliminary Study in Rural China." *Population, Space and Place* 13 (3): 179–91.

Xu, Xiaohe, and Martin K. Whyte. 1990. "Love Matches and Arranged Marriages: A Chinese Replication." *Journal of Marriage and the Family* 52 (3): 709–22.

Xu, Yiyuan, Jo Ann M. Farver, Zengxiu Zhang, Qiang Zeng, Lidong Yu, and Beiying Cai. 2005. "Mainland Chinese Parenting Styles and Parent-Child Interaction." *International Journal of Behavioral Development* 29 (6): 524–31.

Yan, Hairong. 2008. *New Masters, New Servants: Migration, Development and Women Workers in China.* Durham, NC: Duke University Press.

Yan, Yunxiang. 2003. *Private Life under Socialism: Love, Intimacy, and Family Change in a Chinese Village, 1949–1999.* Stanford, CA: Stanford University Press.

Ye, Jingzhong, and Lu Pan. 2011. "Differentiated Childhood: Impacts of Rural Labour Migration on Left-behind Children in China." *Journal of Peasant Studies* 38 (2): 355–77.

Yi, Qingchun. 2006. "Zhongguo Fuqi De Hunyin Quanli: Yige Bijiao Yanjiu" [Marital Power among Chinese Couples: A Comparative Analysis]. *The Family Status of Chinese Women: Taiwan, Tianjin, Shanghai and Hong Kong Compared,* edited by Qingchun Yi, and Yuhua Chen, 51–82. Beijing: Social Sciences Academic Press. (In Chinese.)

Yi, Qingchun, and Yuhua Chen. 2006. *Zhongguo Funv De Jiating Diwei: Taiwan, Tianjin, Shanghai He Xianggang De Bijiao* [The Family Status of Chinese Women: Taiwan, Tianjin, Shanghai and Hong Kong Compared]. Beijing: Social Sciences Academic Press. (In Chinese.)

Yip, Winnie, and William C. Hsiao. 2015. "What Drove the Cycles of Chinese Health Care Reform." *Health Systems & Reform* 1 (1): 52–61.

Zhan, Heying Jenny, and Rhonda J. Y. Montgomery. 2003. "Gender and Elder Care in China: The Influence of Filial Piety and Structural Constraints." *Gender & Society* 17 (2): 209–29.

Zhang, Chuanhong, and Qijie Gao. 2014. "Impact of Rural-Urban Migration on Gender Relations of Rural-Urban Migrant Households in China." *Journal of Research in Gender Studies* 4 (2): 183–205.

Zhang, Everett. 2011. "China's Sexual Revolution." *Deep China: The Moral Life of the Person: What Anthropology and Psychiatry Tell Us about China*

Today, edited by A. Kleinman, Y. Yan, J. Jun, S. Lee, E. Zhang, et al., 106–51. Berkeley, CA: University of California Press.

Zhang, Jun, and Peidong Sun. 2014. "'When Are You Going to Get Married?' Parental Matchmaking and Middle-Class Women in Contemporary Urban China." *Wives, Husbands, and Lovers: Marriage and Sexuality in Hong Kong, Taiwan, and Urban China*, edited by Deborah S. Davis and Sara L. Friedman, 118–46. Stanford, CA: Stanford University Press.

Zhang, Li. 2007. "Living and Working at the Margin: Rural Migrant Workers in China's Transition Cities." *Marginalisation in China: Perspectives on Transition and Globalisation*, edited by Heather Xiaoquan Zhang, Bin Wu, and Richard Sanders, 81-96. Aldershot: Ashgate.

Zhang, Nana. 2014. "Performing Identities: Women in Rural–Urban Migration in Contemporary China." *Geoforum* 54 (July): 17–27.

Zhou, Minhui, Rachel Murphy, and Ran Tao. 2014. "Effects of Parents' Migration on the Education of Children Left Behind in Rural China." *Population and Development Review* 40 (2): 273–92.

Zhou, Zongkui, Xiaojun Sun, Ya Liu, and Dongming Zhou. 2005. "Nongcun Liushou Ertong Xinli Fazhan Yu Jiaoyu Wenti" [Psychological Development and Education Problems of Children Left in Rural Areas]. *Journal of Beijing Normal University (Social Science Edition)* 187 (1): 71–89. (In Chinese.)

Zhu, Xiujie. 2005. "Nongcun Nvxing Renkou Liudong De Yunshu Jizhi: Shehui Xingbie Shijiao Fenxin" [Restriction Mechanism on Rural Female Migrant Population Flow: An Analysis from Socio-Gender Perspectives]. *Southern Demography* 20 (1): 18–24. (In Chinese.)

Zhu, Yu. 2007. "China's Floating Population and Their Settlement Intention in the Cities: Beyond the Hukou Reform." *Habitat International* 31 (1): 65–76.

Zhu, Yu, and Wenzhe Chen. 2010. "The Settlement Intention of China's Floating Population in the Cities: Recent Changes and Multifaceted Individual-Level Determinants." *Population Space and Place* 16 (4): 253–67.

Zuo, Jiping. 2009. "Rethinking Family Patriarchy and Women's Positions in Presocialist China." *Journal of Marriage and Family* 71 (3): 542–57.

Index

- nuanced, holistic, pluralistic view of masc.
- tea ♀ exp. not ignored - learn about it through men's exp and the ♀ interviews
- identifies trends w/o oversimplifying and maintaining heterogeneous exp.